The Gospel of John:
Discussion and Study Guide

By

Joseph McRae Mellichamp

Thousand Fields Publishing
Johns Creek, Georgia 30097
www.1000fieldspub.com

To Followers of Jesus Who Want to Love Him as John Did

The Gospel of John:
Discussion and Study Guide

THE GOSPEL OF JOHN: DISCUSSION AND STUDY GUIDE
Foreword

One of the most frequently made criticisms of the Bible by its opponents is that the gospel accounts of Jesus are inconsistent and, indeed, often contradictory. You can be sure of two things when you hear such comments: (1) the person making the comment doesn't know what he or she is talking about and (2) what seem to some as contradictory accounts about Jesus are actually accounts which accurately portray different aspects of His character and ministry. In fact, without these four rich and varied portraits of Jesus, we would have an incomplete understanding of who Jesus is and what He intends to accomplish in His Creation.

Before we begin our look at the Gospel of John, let's take a closer at the four gospels together. The first three gospels, Matthew, Mark, and Luke, are called the synoptic gospels— synoptic from the Greek prefix *syn* (together) and noun *optic* (to see); thus, synoptic means to see together or to see alike. What this means is the narratives of the life of Jesus in these three gospels are from a similar perspective. Bible scholars agree that the perspective they employ is a literary genre called historical biography. That is, they are presenting biographical details of Jesus, His life and ministry.

Now suppose three authors today wrote biographies of some famous person, say George Washington. Would we expect or require that they all three included the very same details about Washington's life? No! And more than that, we would expect the three authors all to emphasize different aspects of his life. One might, for example portray him as "The Father of Our Country", another might focus on his military accomplishments, and the third might emphasize his contributions to democracy in general. And we would not be put off by this circumstance in the least nor would we protest that the accounts were inconsistent or contradictory. This is exactly what we find when we examine the gospels. Let's look at the gospel authors and see if we can discover what they were attempting to emphasize in their portrayals of Jesus.

Matthew, the only eyewitness of the three, was a resident of Capernaum in Galilee and a tax collector when he was called by Jesus to follow Him. Here is my speculation on what became of Matthew after the resurrection of Jesus and His ascension into heaven. Tradition tells us that Matthew remained in Jerusalem for about fifteen years after the death and resurrection of Jesus. Jesus died in 30 AD according to our best accounting; thus, this would put Matthew in Jerusalem until 45 or 46 AD. I suggest that Matthew left Jerusalem and joined the believers in Antioch (Syria). He might have even then been compiling a record of the sayings of Jesus, which could have been completed in Antioch in the mid 50s AD time-frame. At the time, Christianity was still primarily a sect closely aligned with Judaism, thus it stands to reason that the sayings would have been written in Aramaic.

While Matthew does not explicitly state his purpose in writing his gospel, it is almost universally agreed that it was to prove that Jesus Christ is the fulfillment of the Messianic predictions of the Old Testament prophets. He gives forty proof passages from the Old Testament in order to make his case, more than any other gospel. That the author is primarily writing to a Jewish audience is apparent from the fact that he makes no attempt to explain Jewish words or customs. Matthew might have left Antioch, possibly with his fellow disciple Thomas, and proceeded to Armenia, Media, and/or Parthia (all provinces in Persia), where he would have composed his Gospel in Greek in the late 50s to early 60s. It would make sense for him to write in Greek as he would have been ministering to Greek speaking people, and Christianity, by this time, had developed into a world religion.

Mark was the son of a woman named Mary who is mentioned in Acts 12:12 as owning a house in Jerusalem which is thought to be the location of the Upper Room. Mark was a cousin of Barnabus (Colossians 4:10) and probably because of this connection traveled with Barnabus and Paul on the first leg of their first missionary journey (46-47 AD). Mark left inexplicably in the midst of the journey and fell out of favor with Paul to the extent that Paul and Barnabus split up. Mark then accompanied Barnabus to Cyprus in 49-52 AD and then associated himself with Peter in the mid 50s AD traveling, scholars believe, to Corinth, Antioch, Babylon, and possibly Rome.

According to Papias, a church father in the second century, Mark was a close associate of Peter, possibly his translator. Papias informs us that Mark recorded the sermons of Peter, which addressed the needs of believers, but the compilation would have been topical and would not have provided a sequential narrative of the life of Jesus. It is thought that the believers in Rome may have encouraged Mark to combine his recorded sermons of Peter into a narrative form resulting in what we call the Gospel of Mark dated in the mid to late 50s AD. Mark's Gospel is a simple, succinct, unadorned, yet vivid account of Jesus' ministry emphasizing more what Jesus did than what he said. It includes wonderfully vivid descriptions, with much detail; his use of present tense vs. past makes for lively action; it is often abrupt and graphic, and miracles are more numerous than parables. A recurrent theme in Mark's account depicts Jesus as a servant (Mark 10:45).

Luke was a physician (Colossians 4:14) and the only Gentile (Colossians 4:10-14) among the gospel writers. Luke states his purpose in writing his narrative in the prolog to the gospel: "Inasmuch as many have undertaken to compile an account of the things accomplished among us, just as they were handed down to us by those who from the beginning were eyewitnesses and servants of the word, it seemed fitting for me as well, having investigated everything carefully from the beginning, to write it out for you in consecutive order, most excellent Theophilus; so that you may know the exact truth about the things you have been taught (Luke 1:1-4)." Luke almost certainly used Mark's gospel as a source and also a source such as Matthew might have compiled of the sayings of Jesus.

Luke is the first of a two part work (Luke-Acts) tracing the historical events surrounding the life and ministry of Jesus and the founding of the early church. Luke's Gospel, probably written in the early 60s, communicates the great truths of Jesus primarily in vivid stories. Luke was written by a Gentile for Gentiles. The author substitutes Greek expressions for nearly all Jewish expressions and seldom appeals to Old Testament prophecy. The author of Luke is more interested in people, especially those in trouble, than in ideas. Luke presents 20 miracle accounts and 28 parables. Luke is the most socially-minded of the gospels. When Jesus spoke in Nazareth, Luke writes He read from Isaiah 61:1,2— citing the poor, broken-hearted, captives, and oppressed.

Thus, we see that the synoptic authors were giving biographical information about Jesus, but they were writing from very different perspectives. Matthew was writing to convince Jewish individuals that Jesus was their promised Messiah. Mark was writing, primarily to a Roman audience, making available the sermons of Peter to address various aspects of life as followers of Jesus. Luke was writing to Gentiles throughout the known world, seeking to give them an accurate, consecutive narrative of the life of Jesus supported by earlier documents and recollections of eyewitnesses. What about John? What was he attempting to accomplish with his gospel account?

By the time John was led by the Spirit of God to write his gospel (85-90 AD), the synoptic gospels had been circulating in the Christian world for 30 or more years. The synoptic gospels, taken together, do a thorough job of establishing what Jesus taught and giving the biographical details of His life and ministry. By this time the real question about Jesus was not, "What He taught?" but "Who was and is He?" And that is exactly what John focuses on in his account. Here is how John describes his purpose: "Many other signs Jesus also performed in the presence of His disciples, which are not written in this book; but these have been written that you may believe that Jesus is the Christ, the Son of God; and that believing you may have life in His name (John 20:30,31)."

John carefully selected seven of the miracles Jesus performed and relates them in narrative form to show the divinity of Jesus, to prove that Jesus is more than a great teacher; to show that Jesus is God, even as He claimed to be again and again. Thus, John's gospel is more than an historical biography; it is an apologetic writing—a defense of the deity of Jesus Christ. When Jesus claimed in John 14:6, "I am the way, and the truth, and the life; no one comes to the Father except through Me", this was possibly the most radical statement ever uttered from the lips of a man. Unless, of course, that Man is God, and then the statement is simply a statement of fact! You must be the judge.

You are going to thoroughly enjoy working your way through this remarkable book. In fact, I would venture to guess that if you seriously read John's gospel following my outlines and answer the questions I have interspersed through the Study Guide, your life will never be the same.

Enjoy the journey. Take some friends along with you.

OVERVIEW OF THE GOSPELS
Rae Mellichamp

Key Verses

- "In the beginning was the Word, and the Word was with God, and the Word was God. He was in the beginning with God. All things came into being through Him, and apart from Him nothing came into being that has come into being." John 1:1-3
- "He is the image of the invisible God, the firstborn of all creation. For by Him all things were created, both in the heavens and on earth, visible and invisible, whether thrones or dominions or rulers or authorities—all things have been created through Him and for Him. He is before all things, and in Him all things hold together. He is also head of the body, the church; and He is the beginning, the firstborn from the dead, so that He Himself will come to have first place in everything. For it was the Father's good pleasure for all the fullness to dwell in Him, and through Him to reconcile all things to Himself, having made peace through the blood of His cross; through Him, I say, whether things on earth or things in heaven. Colossians 1:15-20

Nature of the Gospels

- See attached chart on "Jesus of the Gospels."
- See attached chart on "Comparison of the Gospels."

Application

1. Do you understand that the entire Bible, from Genesis to The Revelation, is about Jesus? It's all about Him. He is the central figure of the Bible and He is the message of the Bible.
2. Do you understand that the four gospels are really four portraits of Jesus each depicting a different manifestation of His divine nature? If we did not have all four gospels, we would have an incomplete picture of Jesus.

3. Do you understand why it is important to know who wrote the gospels and when they were written? A favorite deception of "liberal" scholarship is to "late date" these documents, rendering their message less accurate and reliable.
4. Do you understand the purpose of the Apostle John in writing his gospel and why it would be important for anyone who is searching for answers to life's essential meaning to study this magnificent book?

Jesus of the Gospels

Topic	Matthew	Mark	Luke	John
Portrait [Picture]	King [Palm Sunday]	Servant [Disciples' Feet]	Man [The Well in Samaria]	God [The Transfiguration]
Key Verse	Matthew 2:2	Mark 10:45	Luke 19:10	John 1:1
Author	Matthew (Levi), son of Alphaeus. One of the twelve apostles. A tax collector.	Mark. A disciple of Peter's and probably translator for Peter in Rome.	Luke. A Greek companion of Paul. A physician and, thus, well-educated.	John brother of James, and son of Zebedee. One of the twelve apostles. Possibly a cousin of Jesus.
Date and Place	60's. Probably before Luke.	50's. Probably Rome.	58-60. Probably Caesarea.	85-90. Ephesus.
Purpose	Matthew was written to the Jews to answer their questions about Jesus of Nazareth who claimed to be the Messiah, to prove that He is the King of the Jews.	As Peter's translator, Mark was probably asked by the Roman Christians to write out in Greek Peter's teachings about Jesus.	Luke 1:1-4. Luke's intent was to verify the accuracy of verbal and written records of the life of Jesus and to compile a written, consecutive account.	John 20:30-31. John gives seven miracles which will enable readers to believe that Jesus is the Christ, the Son of God, and have eternal life.
Distinctives	Most systematic, complete record of Jesus' teaching. Cited first in most lists of gospels because of: content and authority.	A gospel for Gentiles and Romans. Focuses more on action. Vivid detail, picturesque descriptions	Highest literary quality of the four gospels. Luke was more interested in people than ideas.	Reminiscences, reflections of an eyewitness. Biography of the growth of John's love and faith.

COMPARISON OF THE GOSPELS

Miracles of Jesus

	Matthew	Mark	Luke	John
Physical and Mental Disorders				
Leper	8:2-3	1:40-42	5:12-13	
Centurion's servant	8:5-13		7:1-10	
Peter's mother-in-law	8:14-15	1:30-31	4:38-39	
Two Gadarenes	8:28-34	5:1-15	8:27-35	
Paralyzed man	9:2-7	2:3-12	5:18-25	
Woman with hemorrhage	9:20-22	5:25-29	8:43-48	
Two blind men	9:27-31			
Man dumb and possessed	9:32-33			
Man with withered hand	12:10-13	3:1-5	6:6-10	
Man blind, dumb, and possessed	12:22		11:14	
Canaanite woman's daughter	15:21-28	7:24-30		
Boy with epilepsy	17:14-18	9:17-29	9:38-43	
Bartimaeus and another blind man	20:29-34	10:46-52	18:35-43	
Deaf and dumb man		7:31-37		
Man possessed in synagogue		1:23-26	4:33-35	
Blind man at Bethsaida		8:22-26		
Man bent double			13:11-13	
Man with dropsy			14:1-4	
Ten lepers			17:11-19	
Malchus' ear			22:50-51	
Official's son at Capernaum				4:46-54
Sick man at Pool of Bethesda				5:1-9
Man born blind				9:1-7
Forces of Nature				
Calming the storm	8:23-27	4:37-41	8:22-25	
Walking on water	14:25	6:48-51		6:19-21
Feeding 5000	14:15-21	6:35-44	9:12-17	6:5-13
Feeding 4000	15:32-38	8:1-9		
Coin in fish's mouth	17:24-27			
Withered fig tree	21:18-22	11:12-14		
Catch of fish			5:1-11	
Water turned to wine				2:1-11
Another catch of fish				21:1-11
Raising the Dead				
Jairus' daughter	9:18-19 9:23-25	5:22-24 5:38-42	8:41-42 8:49-56	
Woman of Nain's son			7:11-15	
Lazarus				11:1-44

Parables of Jesus

	Matthew	Mark	Luke
Lamp under a bushel	5:14-15	4:21-22	8:16, 11:33
Houses on rock and sand	7:24-27		6:47-49
New cloth on an old garment	9:16	2:21	5:36
New wine in old wineskins	9:17	2:22	5:37-38
Sower and soils	13:3-8	4:3-8	8:5-8
Mustard seed	13:31-32	4:30-32	13:18-19
Tares	13:24-30		
Leaven	13:33		13:20-21
Hidden treasure	13:44		
Pearl of great value	13:45-46		
Dragnet	13:47-48		
Lost sheep	18:12-13		15:4-6
Unforgiving servant	18:23-34		
Workers in the vineyard	20:1-16		
Two sons	21:28-31		
Wicked tenants	21:33-41	12:1-9	20:9-16
Invitation to wedding feast	22:1-14		
Ten bridesmaids	25:1-13		
Fig tree as sign of summer	24:32-33	13:28-29	21:29-32
Talents (Matthew), Pounds (Luke)	25:14-30		19:12-27
Sheep and goats	25:31-36		
Growing seed		4:26-29	
Creditor and debtors			7:41-43
Good Samaritan			10:30-37
Friend in need			11:5-8
Rich fool			12:16-21
Alert servants			12:35-40
Faithful steward			12:42-48
Fig tree without figs			13:6-9
Places of honor at wedding feast			14:7-14
Great banquet and reluctant guests			14:16-24
Counting the cost			14:28-33
Lost coin			15:8-10
The prodigal son			15:11-32
Dishonest steward			16:1-8
Rich man and Lazarus			16:19-31
The master and his servant			17:7-10
The persistent widow, unrighteous judge			18:2-5
The Pharisee and the tax collector			18:10-14

Source: Eerdman's Handbook to the Bible. Grand Rapids, MI: William B. Eerdmans Publishing Company. 1973. pp 664-5

CONTENT OF THE GOSPELS
Rae Mellichamp

Key Verses

- "Inasmuch as many have undertaken to compile an account of the things accomplished among us, just as they were handed down to us by those who from the beginning were eyewitnesses and servants of the word, it seemed fitting for me as well, having investigated everything carefully from the beginning, to write it out for you in consecutive order, most excellent Theophilus; so that you may know the exact truth about the things you have been taught." Luke 1:1-4
- "What was from the beginning, what we have heard, what we have seen with our eyes, what we have looked at and touched with our hands, concerning the Word of Life—and the life was manifested, and we have seen and testify and proclaim to you the eternal life, which was with the Father and was manifested to us—what we have seen and heard we proclaim to you also, so that you too may have fellowship with us; and indeed our fellowship is with the Father, and with His Son Jesus Christ. These things we write, so that our joy may be made complete." 1 John 1:1-4

Portraits in the Gospels

- See attached chart on "Jesus of the Synoptic Gospels."
- See attached chart on "Jesus of John's Gospel."

Application

1. Do you understand the distinction between the Synoptics (Matthew, Mark, and Luke) and John's gospel? In what ways are the Synoptics different from John? In what ways are they alike?

2. How would you respond to someone who stated emphatically that none of the four gospels was written by an eyewitness to the events described?

3. John states his purpose in writing his account in John 20:30-31. What is his primary line of evidence to prove to the reader that Jesus is the divine Son of God? Are you personally convinced that He is?

4. Is the book of John an exhaustive account of everything that Jesus said and did during His years on earth? See John 20:30; 21:25

Jesus of the Synoptic Gospels

Topic	Matthew	Mark	Luke
Portrait	King	Servant	Man
Prolog			Luke 1:1-4
Genealogy	Matthew 1:1-17. Joseph Abraham to Joseph		Luke 3:23-38. Mary Adam to Heli (Mary's father)
Characteristics	**Gospel of the King** 1. Seeks to prove that Jesus is the Christ. 128 OT quotes. - Born in Bethlehem. 2:1 - Presented with gifts. 2:11 - Preceded by messenger. 3:1,3 - Son of God. 3:17 - Ministry of miracles. 9:35 - King. 27:37 2. Has a special interest in the church. 16:18; 18:17 3. Has an interest in eschatology, the second coming of Jesus. 4. Has a special interest in the teachings of Jesus, especially about the Kingdom of Heaven. 5-7,10,13,18,24 5. Shows Jesus as a King with power.	**Gospel for Gentiles** 1. Translates Aramaic expressions into Greek. 3:17;15:22 2. Explains Jewish customs. 14:12; 15:42 3. The Law is not mentioned. OT is quoted only once in Mark's part. 4. Gentile sections. Chapters 5-8 **Gospel for Romans** 1. Explanation of a Greek term by a Latin one. 12:42 2. Works of power, authority, patience, endurance. 2:10 3. Forbids a Roman (not Jewish) practice. 10:12 4. The centurion's conclusion. 15:39	**Gospel for Gentiles** 1. Substitutes Greek expressions for nearly all Jewish ones. 2. When quoting OT, uses inclusive verses. 3:6 3. Intended to supply influential Romans solid truth about Jesus. 4. Shows that Jesus was proved innocent of the charge of subversion. 23:14 5. Shows that Jesus associated with all people. 6. Shows that Christianity is neither superstitious nor subversive. 7. Most universal of all gospels. Jesus has compassion for all. 8. Most socially minded gospel. Poor, widows, orphans. 4:16-19

Jesus of the Synoptic Gospels
Continued

Topic	Matthew	Mark	Luke
Portrait	King	Servant	Man

Characteristics (Continued)	The Sermon on the Mount
	
	1. The Beatitudes
	2. Precepts for Kingdom Life
	  - Law of Moses
	  - Law of murder
	  - Law of reconciliation
	  - Law of adultery, divorce
	  - Law of love
	3. Practice of Kingdom Life
	  - Giving
	  - Prayer
	  - Fasting
	  - Money
	  - Anxiety
		Gospel of the Servant
		
		1. Jesus is God's chosen.
		2. He has a mission to establish God's judgment.
		3. His endowment is the Holy Spirit and faith.
		4. He is a combination of greatness and lowliness.
		5. He experiences suffering—bearing our sin.
		6. He redeems Israel and brings light to the Gentiles.
			A Gospel of Prayer
			
			Luke focuses more on prayer than the other gospels.
			1. At His baptism. 3:21
			2. His practice. 5:16
			3. Calling the twelve. 6:12
			4. Peter's confession. 9:18
			5. The transfiguration. 9:28,29
			6. The Lord's prayer. 11:1
			7. For Peter. 22:32

Ending	Matthew 28:18-20. The Great Commission	Mark 16:9-20. Probably not Mark's ending. Original may be lost.	Luke 24:50-53. The ascension of Jesus from the Mt. Of Olives.

8

Jesus of John's Gospel

Topic	John	
Portrait	God	
Prolog	John 1:1-18. In the beginning was the Word, and the Word was with God, and the Word was God.	
Characteristics	Seven Attesting Miracles	"I am" Claims
	1. Turning water into wine. 2:1-11	1. I am the bread of life. 6:35
		2. I am the light of the world. 8:12
	2. Healing the royal official's son. John 4:46-54	3. I am the door. 10:9
		4. I am the good shepherd. 10:11
	3. Healing the paralytic. 5:1-18	5. I am the resurrection. 11:25
		6. I am the way, truth, life. 14:6
	4. Feeding the 5000. 6:1-13	7. I am the vine. 15:1
	5. Walking on water. 6:16-21	Jesus Claimed to be God
	6. Restoring the blind man's sight. 9:1-7	Before Abraham was born, I am. 8:56-59
		Jesus Taught Salvation by Faith
	7. Raising Lazarus from the dead. 11:1-45	I am the resurrection and the life. 11:20-26
Ending	John 21:15-25. Jesus did many other things which if they were written even the world would not contain the books.	

9

INTRODUCTION TO THE GOSPEL OF JOHN
Rae Mellichamp

Who?

John, the Apostle
- Son of Zebedee and Salome? (sister of Mary, thus, aunt of Jesus. Matt. 27:56, Mark 15:40).
- Younger brother of James (executed by Herod Agrippa I in AD 44. Acts 12:1,2).
- Fisherman on the Sea of Galilee with father, brother, and hired servants. Mark 1:19,20
- Disciple of John the Baptist. John 1:35
- Nicknamed *Son of Thunder* by Jesus. Mark 3:19, Luke 9:54, Mark 10:35-40
- One of the inner circle of the disciples of Jesus. Mark 5:37, Matthew 17:1;26:37
- Author of 1,2,3 John and Revelation. Rev 1:1,4,9

External Evidence:
- Polycarp (69?-155? AD). A disciple of John and bishop of Smyrna.
- Irenaeus (140?-202? AD). A disciple of Polycarp, bishop of Lyon, and author of *Against the Heresies.*
- Eusebius (260?-340? AD). Bishop of Caesarea and author of a history of the church until 324.

Internal Evidence:
- Acquainted with Jewish religious beliefs and customs. John 4:9,25; 7:2,27,37,38,42; 10:22,23.
- Detailed knowledge of Palestinian geography. John 1:28; 2:1,12; 3:23.
- Detailed knowledge of Jerusalem and the temple. John 5:2; 9:7 and John 2:14,20; 8:20.
- Intimate knowledge of actions, words and feelings of the Twelve. John 4:27; 6:19; 12:16, 20:2.

- Mentions Simon Peter, Andrew, Philip, Nathaniel, Thomas, Judas and Judas Iscariot by name. This leaves only Matthew, James the Less, Simon the Zealot, and James and John.
- "The disciple whom Jesus loved." John 21:19-24.

What?

The fourth Gospel. See "Overview of John."

Characteristics:
- Most theological Gospel emphasizing the deity of Christ.
- Most precise in terms of places, dates, and times of events.
- Most well written in terms of style, arrangement, arguments, and phrase construction.

When?

85-90 AD

- John Rylands Fragment (117-138 AD). A papyrus fragment found in Egypt which is the earliest known copy of any portion of the New Testament.
- Present tense of John 5:2 may indicate a date earlier than 70 AD when Jerusalem was destroyed by the Romans.

Where?

Strong tradition holds that the book was written in Asia Minor, probably from Ephesus, where John cared for Mary, the mother of Jesus, and was the leader of the church until his death toward the close of the century. Tradition says John wrote this book at the request of Christian friends, and that he agreed to do so only after the church had fasted and prayed for three days.

The book was apparently written to Christians everywhere. By the last part of the second century, this Gospel was well known

11

throughout Christendom: in Africa, Asia Minor, Italy, Gaul, and Syria.

Why?

The writer's purpose is clearly stated in John 20:30,31.

So What?

1. Are you personally satisfied that the Gospel of John was written by the disciple of Jesus whose name was John? Why is this an important consideration in studying this account of the life and ministry of Jesus?
2. One of the arguments for dating the Synoptics in the middle of the first century is that none mentions the destruction of the Temple which occurred in 70 AD. But this argument is never applied to John's gospel. Why do you suppose this is so?
3. Some of the important documents used by "liberal scholars" in assessing the life and ministry of Jesus are the so-called Gnostic Gospels—documents written in the second and third centuries. Do you understand why we prefer to base our understanding of who Jesus is on the canonical gospels—Matthew, Mark, Luke, and John?

OVERVIEW OF JOHN
Rae Mellichamp

Key Verses

- "In the beginning was the Word, and the Word was with God, and the Word was God. He was in the beginning with God. All things came into being through Him, and apart from Him nothing came into being that has come into being. In Him was life, and the life was the Light of men. The Light shines in the darkness, and the darkness did not comprehend it." John 1:1-5
- "Therefore many other signs Jesus also performed in the presence of the disciples, which are not written in this book; but these have been written so that you may believe that Jesus is the Christ, the Son of God; and that believing you may have life in His name." John 20:30-31

Major Events (Locations) in John

- See attached bookchart on "The Gospel of John." (page 15)
- See attached map of "Palestine in Christ's Time." (page 16)

Application

1. A bookchart of a book of the Bible can give one a quick overview of the material covered in the book. Was the bookchart included helpful to you in overviewing John's gospel? If so, how?
2. In studying and applying God's word, one needs to be an historian as well as a cartographer. Has our focus on geographical locations been helpful? Do you think it would be useful to make frequent reference to maps in studying the Word?
3. If you were reading along in some book of the Bible and came across a place name for which you had no clue how to locate on a map, what would you do? Skipping over it is not an acceptable answer.

4. Jesus traversed the region of Palestine several times during His ministry. There were no buses, trains, restaurants, or McDonalds and very few inns which He probably didn't frequent. What conclusion may we draw from this?

The Gospel of John Bookchart

Periods in the Ministry of Jesus

Section	Chapter	Location
Pro-log	Ch 1. The Word	Bethany Beyond Jordan 1:28
Consideration	Ch 2. Wedding at Cana. M-1	Cana 2:1 / Capernaum 2:12 / Jerusalem 2:13
Consideration	Ch 3. Nicodemus, Baptizing	Judea 3:22
Consideration	Ch 4. Samaritan Woman. M-2	Sychar 4:4 / Cana 4:46
Contro-versy	Ch 5. Healing at Bethesda. M-3	Jerusalem 5:1
Contro-versy	Ch 6. 5000 Fed, Bread. M-4,M-5,IAM-1	Sea of Galilee 6:1 / Capernaum 6:17
Conflict	Ch 7. Living Water	Galilee 7:1 / Jerusalem 7:10
Conflict	Ch 8. Adulterous Woman. IAM-2	Mt of Olives 8:1 / Temple 8:2
Conflict	Ch 9. A Blind Man. M-6	
Conflict	Ch 10. The Good Shepherd. IAM-3,IAM-4	Bethany Beyond Jordan 10:40
Conflict	Ch 11. Lazarus. M-7,IAM-5	Bethany 11:17 / Ephraim 11:54
Crisis	Ch 12. The Anointing, Light	Bethany 12:1 / Jerusalem 12:12
Crisis	Ch 13. Washing Feet, Betrayal	
Conference	Ch 14. Truth, The Holy Spirit I. IAM-6	
Conference	Ch 15. The Vine. IAM-7	
Conference	Ch 16. The Holy Spirit II	
Conference	Ch 17. Farewell Prayer	
Consummation	Ch 18. Arrest and Trial	
Consummation	Ch 19. Crucifixion	
Consummation	Ch 20. Resurrection	
Epi-log	Ch 21. Final Instructions	Sea of Galilee 21:1

15

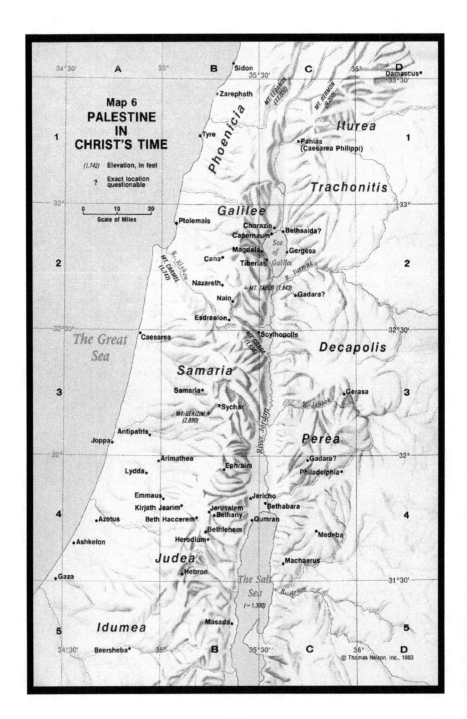

Map 6
PALESTINE
IN
CHRIST'S TIME

(1,742) Elevation, in feet

? Exact location
   questionable

0   10   20
Scale of Miles

The Great Sea

Phoenicia

Iturea

Trachonitis

Sidon
Zarephath
Tyre
Panias
(Caesarea Philippi)

Galilee

Ptolemais
Chorazin
Capernaum
Bethsaida?
Sea of Galilee
Magdala
Gergesa
Cana
Tiberias
Nazareth
+MT. TABOR (1,843)
Nain
Gadara?
Esdraelon

Caesarea
Scythopolis

Decapolis

Samaria

Samaria
Gerasa
Sychar
MT. GERIZIM + (2,890)
R. Jabbok

Antipatris
Joppa

Perea

Arimathea
Gadara?
Lydda
Philadelphia

Emmaus
Jericho
Kirjath Jearim
Bethabara
Jerusalem
Azotus
Bethany
Beth Haccerem
Qumran
Bethlehem
Medeba
Herodium

Judea

Machaerus
Gaza
Hebron
The Salt Sea
(−1,300)
R. Arnon

Idumea

Masada
Beersheba

© Thomas Nelson, Inc., 1983

16

JOHN 1

Prolog. John 1:1-18

- Jesus.
    - The Word. Greek form:
        - logos (log'-os); something said (including the thought); by implication a topic (subject of discourse), specifically (with the article in John) the Divine Expression (i.e. Christ).
        - lego (leg'-o); a primary verb; properly, to "lay" forth, i.e. (figuratively) relate in words usually of systematic or set discourse.
    - Eternal. He has always existed.
    - Omnipotent. He created all things.
    - Light. He is the source of life.
    - Co-equal. He is God.
- John the Baptist.
    - His job. What he did.
    - His person. Who he was.
    - His message. What he preached.
- Jesus' Reception.
    - The world did not recognize Him.
    - The Jews did not accept Him.
    - Some *believe* and *receive* Him; they are reborn:
        - Not physically.
        - Spiritually.
- The Word.
    - The Incarnation. Jesus (God) became flesh and lived among men.
        - Full of grace and truth.
        - Reflecting the glory of God.
    - The Contrast.
        - The Written Word (the law). Leads us to God. (Galatians 3:24)
        - The Living Word (Jesus). Enables us to see God. (John 14:9)

Applications

1. In mathematics, there is a concept known as an *identity*, defined as follows: objects *a* and *b* can be said to be qualitatively identical if *a* and *b* are duplicates, that is, if *a* and *b* are exactly similar in all respects, that is, if *a* and *b* have all qualitative properties in common. John is basically arguing here that Jesus and God are identical in all respects, thus Jesus is God. What attributes of Jesus does John mention?
2. Are you personally satisfied that Jesus is God? Suppose someone suggested to you that Jesus was just a great teacher. How would you respond?
3. In verse 5, John writes, "And the light shines in the darkness and the darkness did not comprehend it." What does he mean by this?
4. In God's plan, was John the Baptist a key figure or did he have a bit part? Of course you answered that he was a key figure. Why?
5. Verse 12 lays out a very significant concept in the Christian faith. What does it mean to *receive* Jesus? What does it mean to *believe* in His name?
6. How can God be superintending His creation as God and living among men as Jesus simultaneously?

John's Testimony. John 1:19-28

- The Inquisition.
    - The interrogators. Priests and Levites from Jerusalem.
    - The questions:
        - Are you the Messiah?
        - Are you Elijah?
        - Are you the Prophet? Deuteronomy 18:15
        - Then who are you?
    - The reply: A messenger. Isaiah 40:3
- A Diversion.
    - A follow-up question. From whom is your authority?
    - The reply:

- My baptism is symbolic.
- The Messiah is coming!

Applications

1. In Matthew 21:23-27, the chief priests and elders came to Jesus and asked Him the same question they had asked John the Baptist, "By what authority are You doing these things?" Why is this such an important question? Do you think the leaders knew the true answer? Why or why not?
2. When John the Baptist told the priests and Levites from Jerusalem that the Messiah was coming, why do you suppose there was no reaction from them?

Jesus' Baptism. John 1:29-34

- John the Baptist's announcement.
  - The Lamb of God.
  - The perfect Sacrifice.
- John the Baptist's verification.
  - I saw the Spirit descend upon Him.
  - God had informed me of this sign.
  - This is my testimony!

Applications

1. Is there any indication in the text that John the Baptist's identification of Jesus as the Messiah had any impact upon those present? Why do you suppose this was so?
2. Suppose you had been present at that time. What do you think your own reaction to John the Baptist's revelation might have been?
3. We have a vast amount of evidence today that Jesus is who John claimed He was, yet people still refuse to believe. Why do you think that is?

First Disciples. John 1:35-51

- Andrew (Manly) and John? (God favored). 35-40
  - John the Baptist's recommendation.
  - Andrew and John's response:
    - They followed Him.
    - They questioned Him.
    - They remained with Him.
- Peter (A piece of rock). 41-42
  - Andrew's recommendation.
  - Peter's response:
    - He went to Jesus.
    - He received a new name.
      - Simon. From the Hebrew (shaw-mah') to hear intelligently with the implication of attention, obedience.
      - Cephas. Of Aramaic origin, the rock.
- Phillip (Fond of horses). 43-44
  - Jesus' call.
  - Philip's response:
    - He followed Jesus.
    - He brought Nathanael.
- Nathanael/Bartholomew? (Given of God). 45-49
  - Philip's recommendation.
    - We have found the Messiah.
    - Jesus of Nazareth, Son of Joseph.
  - Nathanael's response:
    - Skepticism. "Can anything good ...?"
    - Interest. He went to investigate.
    - Belief. "You are the Son of God ..."
- Jesus' Prediction. John 1:50-51

Applications

1. Some scholars argue that Jesus' call to Peter and Andrew in Mark 1:16,17 and Matthew 4:18,19 preceded the events related in John 1. How would you respond to such a statement?

20

2. Suppose you had been present during these days. Do you think you might have been called to follow Jesus? You have, of course, been called to follow Him in these present days. Are you following Him?
3. Who were the first people to tell others about Jesus? Did any of them have any formal training in evangelism? What are the implications for us from this?
4. Have you ever told anyone about Jesus? From this account, it looks pretty easy. You go tell someone what you know about Jesus and they respond in faith. Will it always be this way? What happens when people don't accept Him?

JOHN 2

The Wedding at Cana. John 2:1-11

- The Guests.
  - Jesus.
  - His mother.
  - His disciples.
  - Others.
- A Problem.
  - Mary: They have no wine.
  - Jesus: It is not My time.
  - Mary: Do what He says.
- The Solution.
  - Fill six large jars with water.
  - Draw some out and sample.
- The Result.
  - Great wine.
  - Impressed witnesses.
    - Servants.
    - Headwaiter.
    - Bridegroom.
  - Believing disciples.

Applications

1. Do you believe Jesus actually turned water into wine? Why isn't any other explanation for this first miracle reasonable?
2. Why do you suppose that people reading this account today try so hard to find an alternative explanation for the simple thing Jesus did?
3. What does this incident say to you about the ability of Jesus to supply any need you might have in your own life?

At Capernaum. John 2:12

- Who.
  - Jesus.
  - His mother and His brothers
  - His disciples.
- What?
- Why?

Applications

1. Where did Jesus' mother and His brothers live? (Hint: Mark 6:1-4)
2. What did His brothers do for a living?

The Temple in Jerusalem. John 2:13-25

- The Setting.
  - The Temple.
  - At Passover. 1st
- The Actors.
  - Jesus.
  - Moneychangers.
  - His disciples.
  - The Jews.
- The Action.
  - A scourge.
  - A scourging.
  - A warning!
- The Interrogation.
  - What sign? (What is Your authority?)
  - Destroy this temple, I will raise it up.
- The Result.
  - Many believed then.
  - His disciples later.
    - Believed in the Scriptures.
    - Remembered His words.

23

-   Jesus trusted no one.

Applications

1. Have you ever been outraged by the way people treat the holy things of the Lord? By the way people use His name in vain. By the way people treat the Sabbath?
2. What would be a proper response to such situations or circumstances? Would it be easy to do more harm than good? In what way?
3. Do you believe the Scriptures? Do you remember His words? What might you do to assist yourself in these two important tasks of a follower of Jesus?

JOHN 3

Jesus and Nicodemus. John 3:1-15

- Nicodemus.
  - His person.
    - A Pharisee.
    - A ruler.
    - A recluse?
  - His preamble.
    - You have come from God.
    - Your signs are proof.
- The Exchange.
  - Jesus' response.
    - Unless one is born again,
    - One cannot see the Kingdom.
  - Nicodemus' reply.
    - How can one be born again?
    - One can't be reborn physically?
  - Jesus' answer.
    - Physical vs. spiritual birth.
    - The spiritually reborn.
  - Nicodemus perplexed.
  - Jesus' elaboration.
    - You should understand.
    - You have rejected My witness.
    - Earthly vs. heavenly things.
      - Moses lifted up the serpent.
      - The Son must be lifted up.

Applications

1. Why do you suppose Nicodemus came to Jesus as he did? Have you ever come to Jesus as Nicodemus did?
2. Several years ago, Chuck Colson, of Watergate fame, wrote a book titled *Born Again* (Old Tappan, NJ: Fleming H. Revell Company, 1976). Many people object to this phrase or belittle

it. What is the similarity between modern day critics and Nicodemus?
3. Jesus chastises Nicodemus for being a teacher of the Jews and yet not understanding the most elemental spiritual things. What about you? What is your level of understanding of spiritual things? What do you need to do in order to beef up your understanding?

Jesus and Men. John 3:16-21

- The Son. 16,17
    - Came to give eternal life.
    - Came not for judgment.
- Men. 18-21
    - Those who believe.
        - Are not judged.
        - Come to the light.
        - Practice the truth.
    - Those who do not believe.
        - Are judged already.
        - Avoid the light.
        - Practice evil.

Applications

1. Jesus describes two classes of people in these verses—those who believe and those who don't. What belief is He describing here?
2. How much understanding does one have to have in order to be counted among those who believe? Does one have to know everything in the Bible, for example?
3. Which of these two classes describes your current thinking? What are the consequences of your belief?
4. John 3:16 used to be the most well-known Bible verse. Today, that distinction goes to Matthew 7:1, "Judge not, lest you be judged." What does this say about our culture? What does it

say about the relevance of the gospel in these days?

Jesus and John. John 3:22-30

- An Update.
  - Jesus and His disciples.
  - Baptizing in Judea.
- The Focus.
  - The actors.
    - John and his disciples.
    - People being baptized.
  - The location.
    - Aenon near Salim.
    - Jordan River.
  - The time.
    - After Nicodemus' inquiry.
    - Before John's imprisonment.
- The Catalyst.
  - A discussion about purification.
  - A comparison of ministries.
- John's Reply.
  - The facts.
    - All ministry is from God.
    - My witness is faithful.
  - A metaphor.
    - The bridegroom.
    - The bridegroom's friend.
  - The conclusion.
    - My joy is full.
    - Jesus must increase.
    - I, John, must decrease.

Applications

1. John the Baptist had a wonderful understanding of who he was and why he was important in God's plan. What about you? Do

27

you know who you are? Do you know why you are here on planet earth?

2. Having an accurate understanding of oneself is necessary to prevent petty comparisons. How do you handle the success of others? Can you honestly rejoice when a sibling "hits the jackpot?" What about the fellow in the next office? When he got the promotion you were both competing for, how did you respond?

3. How would you characterize yourself in relation to Jesus? Do you see yourself as the bridegroom's friend? Or are you only a vague acquaintance? Do you need to do anything to become better acquainted with the most attractive person of history?

John or John? John 3:31-36

- A Contrast.
  - Jesus.
    - Comes from above.
    - Is above all.
  - John (Men).
    - Is of the earth.
    - Speaks of the earth.
- Jesus' Message.
  - His witness.
    - What He proclaims.
    - How men respond.
  - His work.
    - He speaks God's words.
    - He gives God's Spirit.
  - His motivation.
    - He has all authority.
    - He has the Father's love.
- The Response.
  - John.
    - I affix my seal.
    - God is true.

- Men.
  - Believers are given eternal life.
  - Unbelievers are given eternal wrath.

Applications

1. Have you ever thought about the fact that when Jesus was on earth, He was primarily sharing with people what He had seen and heard as He spent eternity past with the Father and the Spirit? What does this say about the authenticity of His message?
2. The Bible teaches that when a person trusts Christ as Savior, he is indwelt by the Spirit of God who begins the process of sanctification—conforming that individual to the image of Jesus. Can you point to evidence that God's Spirit is indeed resident in you and is at work changing your life?
3. Of course you and I are earthly creatures and we live earthly existences. But we also have a spiritual dimension to our lives and we can think, dream and speak of spiritual things. Is your speech totally focused on earthly things? To what extent should our speech be more focused on heavenly issues?

JOHN 4

Jesus and the Woman at the Well. John 4:1-38

- The Situation.
    - Change of venue.
        - The reason.
        - The route.
        - The rest.
    - Time of day.
    - Cast of characters
        - Jesus.
        - A Samaritan woman.
        - The disciples.
- The Exchange.
    - Assessing the interest.
        - The cultural issue.
        - The sexual issue.
    - Sowing the seed.
        - Woman: Jews and Samaritans.
        - Jesus: Living water.
    - Explaining the benefits.
        - Woman: Are You greater than Jacob?
        - Jesus: Living water revisited.
    - Dealing with personal issues.
        - Woman: Give me this water.
        - Jesus: Get your husband.
    - Telling the truth.
        - Woman: I don't have one.
        - Jesus: You have had five.
    - Dealing with spiritual issues.
        - Woman: You are a prophet.
            - Our worship.
            - Your worship.
        - Jesus: True worship.
            - Your worship.
            - Our worship.

30

- Presenting the Truth.
  - Woman: The Messiah.
  - Jesus: I am He.
- The Reactions.
  - The woman's response.
    - She leaves the well hastily.
    - She questions the villagers intently.
  - The disciples' reaction.
    - Puzzled but silent.
    - Concerned but demanding.
  - The Messiah's instruction.
    - My food.
    - My harvest.
      - Ripe fruit.
      - Reapers.
      - Sowers.

Applications

1. Why do you suppose John included this episode in his gospel? It is neither one of the seven miracle accounts nor one of the "I am" statements which form the "backbone" of John's gospel. So why did he choose to include it?
2. In engaging the Samaritan woman, Jesus initiated the conversation by asking her for a drink of water—something that would not have been done in the cultural situation. Why did He do this? What risks did He assume in asking?
3. Do you ever initiate conversations with strangers with the intention of moving from everyday chat to discussing spiritual issues? Do you make it a practice of trying to determine where people are in relation to Christ in order that you might engage them? Can you share some examples?
4. Can you see the progress of the woman as the conversation flows? Can you see her moving from light conversation to interest in spiritual issues to raising her defenses to understanding her need for a Savior?

31

Jesus and the Samaritan Villagers. John 4:39-42

- Initial Belief: The Woman's Word.
- Maturing Belief: The Peoples' Experience.
  - They heard.
  - They understood.
- The Outcome.
  - The conclusion: "Savior of the World."
  - The result: Many from the village believed.

Applications

1. The Samaritan villagers at first believed in Jesus because of the testimony of the woman, but as they saw and heard Jesus, the basis of their faith changed. What is the basis of your faith? Have you experienced first-hand the touch of Jesus in your life?
2. What do you suppose would have happened in the village if the woman had simply gone and fetched her husband as Jesus had asked without sharing her experience with Jesus with the villagers? How much did the woman know about Jesus when she first shared with her neighbors?
3. What does John tell us about the activities of the disciples in all of this? Do you think they were really into reaching the Samaritans? Or do you think they viewed the Samaritans as a hindrance and were ready to hit the trail for Galilee?
4. Was this episode accidental? If not, what does it tell us about the sovereignty of God in relation to people anywhere, even in Samaria, who truly want to know Him?

Jesus and the Galilean Villagers. John 4:43-45

- Jesus' Testimony.
- Galilean Reception.

Applications

1. Can you explain the apparent contradiction between Jesus' testimony that a prophet is without honor in his own country and the reception of Him by the Galileans? Do you suppose He performed miracles in their midst as a result of their reception?
2. What does it mean, "the Galileans received Him?" Is this simply a description of their hospitality toward Him as a visitor in their region or does it imply a deeper level of spiritual belief? No speculation allowed here.

Jesus and the Royal Official's Son. John 4:46-54

- The Locations.
  - Cana.
  - Capernaum.
- The People.
  - The royal official.
  - The official's son.
- The Request.
  - Come heal my son.
  - Come before he dies.
- The Admonition.
  - You require signs and wonders.
  - You only need simple faith.
- The Response.
  - The official believed Jesus.
  - The official departed Cana.
  - The official received word.
  - The official believed in Jesus.

Applications

1. Romans 10:17 says, "So faith comes from hearing, and hearing by the word of Christ." Can you see this principle illustrated in the Samaritan village? In the situation with the official's son? How does this principle apply in your own life?

2. What do you make of the fact that the official traveled from Capernaum to Cana to speak to Jesus? How far are you willing to travel to interact with Jesus? Across the living room? Across the town? Across the country? To another country?
3. What are some possible explanations for the initial obedience of the official to Jesus' instructions? What does it mean when John says, "he himself believed and his whole household?"
4. How much of this episode was apparent to the disciples? What do you suppose was going through their minds as this situation played itself out before them?

JOHN 5

Jesus and the Paralytic. John 5:1-9

- The Situation.
  - The time.
    - After Galilee.
    - At the Passover.
    - On the Sabbath.
  - The location.
    - In Jerusalem.
    - By the Sheep Gate.
    - At the Bethesda Pool.
  - The characters.
    - Jesus.
    - The disciples?
    - A man.
      - Paralyzed, immovable.
      - Thirty-eight years.
- The Miracle.
  - Jesus was involved.
    - He saw.
    - He knew.
    - He asked.
  - The man was defeated.
    - No one helps me.
    - Others beat me.
  - Jesus acted.
    - The command.
    - The result.

Applications

1. What was Jesus doing at the Pool of Bethesda? It may have been on His way from Galilee, but only if He came back through Samaria. Do you think this likely, given His recent movements?

2. Why would Jesus concern Himself with just one man when there were obviously many others at the pool waiting for the waters to be stirred?

Further Instructions. John 5:10-18

- From the Jews.
  - An unfeeling critique.
    - Their admonition.
    - Their basis.
  - An uninformed response.
    - My authority—the man who healed me.
    - My intention—walking and carrying.
  - An unsympathetic query.
  - An unsatisfactory answer.
- From Jesus.
  - Jesus sought the man.
    - Jesus found him.
    - Jesus warned him.
  - The man sought the Jews.
  - The Jews persecuted Jesus.
  - Jesus instructed the Jews.
    - My Father is working.
    - I Myself am working.
  - The Jews intensified their opposition.
    - For His breaking the Sabbath.
    - For equating Himself with God.

Applications

1. Can you explain why the man left Jesus without ascertaining who He was or thanking Him for His gift of healing? How often do we ask God for something and fail to acknowledge His grace when He answers our prayer?
2. Why do you suppose the Jews admonished the man for working on the Sabbath? Do you suppose they knew him? Do you think they were really concerned about the Sabbath? Are you

36

concerned at all with observing the Sabbath or is that just OT stuff?

3. The man had been paralyzed for thirty-eight years? What do you suppose his reaction was to their admonition? Is this inferred from the text?

4. Do you think Jesus observed the Sabbath? This is one of the texts from which we infer that works of necessity and works of mercy are acceptable activities on the Sabbath? Did the Jews get it? Do you?

5. Many today think Jesus is merely a great teacher. But here He clearly claims to be much more than that. He actually claims to be God. Did the Jews understand what He was telling them? How do you know?

The Work of the Son. John 5:19-29

- The Son Watches the Father.
- The Father Shows the Son.
- The Son Executes Judgment.
  - To be honored.
  - To reveal destiny.
    - Evil deeds—to judgment.
    - Good deeds—to life.

The Will of the Son. John 5:30

The Witness of the Son. John 5:31-37

- Jesus' Witness.
- John's Witness.
- Jesus' Works.
- God's Witness.
  - At His baptism.
  - At the Transfiguration.
  - At the crucifixion.

Applications

1. What does Jesus mean when He says, "The Son can do nothing of Himself, unless it is something He sees the Father doing?"
2. What are the implications of verse 21? Are you impacted at all by this statement or is this just some theological platitude that really has no bearing on you at all?
3. In verse 30, Jesus says, "I do not seek My own will, but the will of Him who sent Me." Would you agree if that was good enough for the Son of God, it ought to be good enough for you? How does one discover the will of God to follow it?
4. In this passage, Jesus mentions four lines of evidence that corroborate who He is. Suggest some specific examples of each and relate how these things have affected your own faith in Him as the Son of God.

The Conclusion of the Son. John 5:38-47

- Jesus' Assessment of Them.
  - You don't have His word in You.
  - You don't have His love in you.
  - You don't seek His glory.
- Their Response to Him.
  - You don't believe Me.
  - You search the Scripture futilely.
  - You won't come to Me.
- Their Judgment before God.
  - Moses.
    - Was their hope.
    - Will be their accuser.
  - Moses' writings.
    - Believe them, believe Me.
    - Reject them, reject Me.

Applications

1. Does Jesus assessment of the Jews also apply to you? Do you have God's word in you? What does that mean? Do you have God's love in you? Can others see it? Do you seek His glory—or the glory of men instead?
2. What is your response on a personal level to Jesus? Do you believe Him? Do you search the Scripture—at all? Have you personally come to Him and bowed before Him with your life?
3. What is your hope? Membership in a church? The faith of your fathers? Will the Scriptures accuse you when you stand before God?

JOHN 6

Jesus Feeds Five Thousand. John 6:1-15

- The Situation.
  - The time.
    - After the Sabbath healing.
    - After ministry in Galilee.
  - The location.
    - The Sea of Galilee (Tiberias).
    - On a mountain.
    - A place with much grass.
    - A place near villages.
  - The characters.
    - Jesus.
    - His disciples.
    - 5000 men.
- Fourth Miracle.
  - Jesus' purpose.
    - To test the disciples.
    - To expose the multitudes.
  - Philip flounders.
    - An intentional question.
    - An incomplete answer.
  - Andrew agonizes.
    - A hurried inventory.
    - A hurried dismissal.
  - Jesus provides.
    - Instructions.
    - Invocation.
    - Invigoration.
  - People experience.
    - They were satisfied.
    - There was surplus.
  - Crowd reaction.
    - He is the Prophet.
    - He will be King.

40

Applications

1. Jesus did not perform miracles to entertain the crowds. Do you see that the feeding of the 5000 was an intentional act of instruction? Can you think of a situation in the gospels in which He articulated this principle? (Hint: Matthew 4, Luke 4)
2. What does this event say about the ability of Jesus to meet the needs of your life—physical, financial, and emotional? Can you think of a reference where He clearly taught this principle? (Hint: Matthew 6:33)

The Disciples on Their Own. John 6:16-21

- The Situation.
  - The time—evening.
  - The location.
    - In a fishing boat.
    - Crossing to Capernaum.
    - Half-way home.
  - The problem.
    - They were ahead of Jesus.
    - They were confronting difficulty.
- His Solution.
  - He came to them.
  - He reassured them.
  - He joined them.
  - He transported them.

Applications

1. Some Biblical scholars explain this event by suggesting that Jesus walked out to the boat on a sandbar. What do you think of this theory?
2. This account illustrates the problem of getting ahead of Jesus—of not waiting on Him. Can you think of a circumstance in your life when you struck out on your own and got in trouble for not

waiting on Jesus? Would you share it with the group?

Jesus and the Five Thousand. John 6:22-40

- The Situation.
    - The crowd.
    - Their assessment.
        - No Jesus.
        - No disciples.
        - No boats.
    - New arrivals.
- The Dialog.
    - First interchange.
        - Jesus. "You seek Me."
            - Wrong motive.
            - Right motive.
        - Crowd. "What should we do?"
        - Jesus. "Believe Me."
    - Second interchange.
        - Crowd. "Show us a sign."
            - Moses gave us manna.
            - What sign do You give?
        - Jesus.
            - The bread of Moses.
            - The bread of God.
    - Third interchange.
        - Crowd. "Give us this bread."
        - Jesus.
            - "I am the bread."
            - If you believe:
                - You will never hunger or thirst.
                - I will not cast you out.
                - I will raise you up on the last day.
                - I will give you eternal life.

Applications

1. Was Jesus impressed at the persistence of the crowd in determining where He was and going to Him? Rather than praising them on their diligence, what was His response to them when they found Him? Was He justified in this reaction?
2. Many people today follow Jesus for the benefits they may gain from Him—extreme examples of this we characterize as the *prosperity* gospel. Do you know people like this? Are you aware of ministries that encourage this sort of thing?
3. Obviously, there are many benefits of following Jesus, not the least of which is the promise of eternal life, but also of an abundant life in the here and now. How can we reconcile our motives, so that we don't follow Him from purely selfish motives?

Jesus Instructs the Jews. John 6:41-51, 59

- Motivation for Instruction.
  - Mumbling about His message.
  - Grumbling against His genealogy.
- Substance of Instruction.
  - Coming to Jesus.
    - One must be drawn by God.
    - One must be taught by God.
    - One must hear and learn from God.
  - Seeing the Father.
  - Partaking of Jesus.
    - The bread of Moses—physical bread.
    - The bread of life—spiritual bread.
- Location of Instruction.

Jesus Clarifies His Instruction. John 6:52-59

- Motivation for Clarification.
- Substance of Clarification.
  - Flesh and Blood: Disposition.

- Eat and drink.
- Abide in Me.
  - Flesh and Blood: Contribution.
    - Eternal life.
    - Resurrection.

Jesus Anticipates Defections. John 6:60-65

- Motives for Defection.
  - Difficult statements.
  - Unreceptive minds.
- Recognition of Discontent.
  - Revealing attitudes.
    - Grumbling.
    - Stumbling.
  - Reinforcing agents.
    - Visions of heaven.
    - Words of spirit and life.
  - Resulting activity.
    - Some won't believe.
    - One will betray.
  - Restoring agent.

Jesus Reassures His Disciples. John 6:66-71

- Movement of Defectors
  - No longer present.
  - No longer believe.
- Questioning the Twelve.
- Answering for All.
  - Whom would we follow?
  - You have the words.
  - We have believed.
- Assessing the Twelve.
  - All chosen.
  - One wanting.

Applications

1. In the concluding verses of John 6, Jesus faces a rebellion as a result of His teaching. Do you think He was surprised by the reaction of the crowd? Or do you think He was intentionally trying to thin the crowds? Explain.
2. The teachings of Jesus and therefore of Christianity are not for intellectual midgets. Are you challenged by the things you read in Scripture? What is your response to hard or difficult teaching? Do you just throw up your hands and blindly accept or do you dig until you begin to understand?
3. Jesus speaks of His body and blood as necessary for life and for eternal life. Do you understand what He is saying here? Suppose a seeker came to you and asked you to explain what Jesus is teaching in this passage. How would you communicate these important truths to someone with virtually no background or understanding of spiritual truth?

JOHN 7

Jesus and His Brothers. John 7:1-9

- The Setting.
  - Galilee. Safety.
  - Judea. Danger.
- The Time.
  - After hard lessons.
  - At the Feast of Tabernacles.
- The Debate.
  - His brothers. "Go to Judea."
    - Display Your works.
    - Increase Your market.
    - "Don't count on us."
  - His response. "You go ahead."
    - You conform and are accepted.
    - I oppose and am hated.
    - "Don't wait for Me."

Applications

1. We are told in Mark 6:3 that Jesus had four brothers: James, Joses (Joseph), Judas (Jude), and Simon. At this stage of His ministry they were probably His worst critics. What do you know about their ultimate feelings toward Him?
2. We know, of course, that Jesus lived a perfect life, never sinning. How can you explain His telling His brothers to go ahead without Him—"I do not go up to this feast because My time has not yet fully come?"

The Crowds Await. John 7:10-13

- The Situation.
  - Jerusalem.
  - The Temple.

- The Crowds. "Where is He?"
  - He is a good man.
  - He leads us astray.
  - No one spoke openly.

Six Questions Concerning Jesus. John 7:14-36

- "How Has He Become Learned?"
  - My teaching.
    - Not Mine.
    - My Father's.
  - Your response.
    - Do His will.
    - Know His teaching.
  - My endorsement.
    - Seeking My own glory?
    - Seeking the Father's glory?
  - Your obedience.
    - You break the law.
    - You seek to kill Me.
- "Who Seeks to Kill You?"
  - My offense.
    - One deed.
    - On the Sabbath.
  - Your reaction.
    - You all marvel.
    - You are angry.
  - Your offense.
    - You work on the Sabbath.
    - You judge on appearance.
- "Is He the One They Seek to Kill?"
  - He speaks publicly.
  - They say nothing.
- "Do They Know That He is the Christ?"
  - Their conclusion.
    - We know where this man is from.
    - We don't know where the Christ is from.

- His correction.
  - You know Me and My origin.
  - You do not know who sent Me.
    - I know Him.
    - I am from Him.
- Their response.
  - They tried to seize Him.
  - They were prevented.
- "The Christ Won't Perform More Signs Than This Man?"
  - The leaders act.
    - Heard the crowds muttering.
    - Sent officers to seize Him.
  - Jesus predicts.
    - I return to Him who sent Me.
    - You will seek and not find.
    - You can't come where I go.
- "Where Does He Intend to Go?"
  - Will He go to the dispersion?
  - What does this statement mean?

Applications

1. The crowd certainly asked a number of questions (six here alone) about Jesus. Do you suppose they were really listening to His answers? Or were they just raising smokescreens like many do today?
2. How can you tell the difference between someone who is asking sincere questions and someone who is just trying to derail a conversation? Do insincere questions deserve and answer? Why, then, does Jesus try to explain Himself?
3. At one point in this episode, the crowds ask the question, "Do they (their leaders) know that He is the Christ?" The leaders obviously knew that Jesus was no ordinary man. How much do you think they really knew? If they knew He was God, an they misled the people, do they deserve condemnation?

Jesus Teaches on the Last Day. John 7:37-44

- Jesus' Teaching.
  - Input: Come to Me and drink.
  - Output: Rivers of living water.
    - Jesus. Present provision to believers.
    - Holy Spirit. Future provision to believers.
- Crowd Reaction. Division.
  - He is the Prophet.
  - He is the Christ.
  - He is not the Christ.
    - The Christ will be from Bethlehem.
    - The Christ will be from David.
  - He must be taken.

Applications

1. Do you think Jesus' sermon was appropriate for the occasion? Remember it was the Feast of Tabernacles they were celebrating. Can you think of some ways during our holidays that you might turn the attention of friends and family toward Jesus?
2. How could the people have made such a big mistake in assuming that Jesus was not from Bethlehem when today we know for sure where He was born?
3. There is much division today over who Jesus really is. Some think Him to be a prophet (Muslims). Some think Him to be a great teacher (professors). Some think him to be a figment invented by His disciples (liberal scholars). Can you argue forcefully that Jesus is God?

Religious Leaders Strategize in Response. John 7:45-53

- Officers Report.
  - Empty-handed.
  - Awe-struck.

- Pharisees React.
  - You have been deceived.
  - Have others been deceived?
    - Rulers who should know better?
    - Commoners do not know better.
- Nicodemus Resists.
  - Proper judgment.
  - Inaccurate facts.
- Everyone Disperses.

Applications

1. Why were the Pharisees so concerned that none of the officers, rulers, or others believe in Jesus? What difference would a few stray followers every now and then possibly matter to them?
2. We learn in Scripture that many of the rulers (John 12:42-43) and priests (Acts 6:7) were believing in Him. Do you understand why it would be a dangerous thing for any of the rulers or priests to confess their faith in Jesus? What hardships might you encounter if you made a strong stand for Him in your family? At work? In your social circle?
3. We can now appreciate the courage that it took for Nicodemus to address the leaders as he did here. How can you account for his courage? (Hint John 3)

JOHN 8

Jesus and the Adulterous Woman. John 8:1-11

- The Setting.
  - Early in the morning.
  - Teaching in the Temple.
- The Characters.
  - Jesus, His disciples.
  - All the people.
  - Scribes and Pharisees.
  - A woman.
- The Question.
  - Scribes and Pharisees.
    - The offense: adultery.
    - The penalty: stoning.
    - The test: "What do You say?"
  - Jesus.
    - Initial response: doodling?
    - Forced response: "He who is without sin …"
    - Ultimate response: doodling?
- The Reaction.
  - Scribes and Pharisees.
    - They departed.
    - Oldest (wisest?) first.
  - The people: watched.
  - The woman.
    - "Who accuses you?"
    - "Go, sin no more."

Applications

1. You may have a marginal note to the effect that this story, although probably authentic, is omitted in many manuscripts and may not have originally been a part of John's Gospel. Regardless, we may draw from the story some forceful principles about Christian behavior. Can you suggest some?

51

2. The Jewish leaders during this phase of the ministry of Jesus went to great lengths to try to trap Him in a situation in order to accuse Him of some serious violation of their law. Here they are at their best. What is your opinion of the wisdom of Jesus after reading of this particular encounter?

3. Having considered this passage, is there anything you need to change about the way you relate to others? The standard to which you would hold others. The necessity of showing mercy to others even as you have been shown mercy by the Lord?

Jesus and the Pharisees. John 8:12-20

- The Setting.
  - Another time: new audience.
  - Another place: the treasury.
- The Issue.
  - Jesus: "I am the light of the world."
  - Pharisees: A question of identity.
    - "You bear witness of Yourself."
    - "Your witness is not true."
  - Jesus: The nature of identity.
    - True vs. False identity.
      - I know: My origin/destination.
      - You don't know: My origin/destination.
    - True vs. false judgment.
      - I and My Father: judge the heart.
      - You judge the externals.
- The Question.
  - Pharisees: "Where is Your Father?"
  - Jesus.
    - "You know neither Me nor My Father."
    - "If you know Me, you know Him."

Applications

1. Here we have the second "I am" statement by Jesus. This statement mirrors John 1:9. What does Jesus mean by this?

Explain how Jesus provides light for your own life. What about people who don't know Him; do you see how they can be as they are?

2. The Jews put a lot stock in outward appearances. They were big on ancestors; where a person was from, etc. But then, so do we. Do you have a problem with judging people by the way they look; by how they dress? If so, how can you address this?

3. Jesus would later tell His disciples "If you knew me, you would know the Father." Based on this principle, how well would you say you know the Father? How does one get to know Jesus? Do you need to respond to this in any way?

The Pharisees and Jesus (Continued). John 8:21-30

- Opening Arguments.
  - Jesus.
    - "I will go away, you will seek Me."
    - "You will die, you can't come."
  - Pharisees.
    - "Will He kill Himself?"
    - "We would not go there."
- Ongoing Dialog.
  - Jesus.
    - Origins.
      - I am from above, I'm not of this world.
      - You are from below, you are of this world.
    - Destiny.
      - Unbelief results in death.
      - Belief results in life.
  - Pharisees: "Who are You?"
- Closing Arguments.
  - Jesus.
    - Remember My instruction.
    - Hear My credentials.
      - My source.
      - My teaching.

- Consider My nature.
  - I do nothing on My own initiative.
  - I do things that please God.
    - Pharisees: Many believed.

Applications

1. We read in Hebrews and other places in Scripture that we are aliens here on planet earth—this is not our home. Jesus knew this well—He came from heaven. What about you? Are you of the world? Are you attached to it? Attracted to it?
2. Here the people ask Jesus one of life's most significant questions, "Who are you?" Suppose a friend or family member came to you and asked you this question. Would you be able to tell him or her who Jesus is? Has anyone ever asked?
3. Jesus was big on living a life pleasing to the Father. In fact, He made pleasing the Father His top life priority. What about you? Is it worth it? Let's face it, following Jesus is not easy. We risk rejection, being misunderstood, ridiculed, criticized. Why bother?

Jesus and the Jews. John 8:31-47

- True Disciples.
  - You abide in My word.
  - You shall know truth.
- False Security.
  - We are Abraham's offspring.
  - We have never been enslaved.
  - Why do You talk of freedom?
- True Freedom.
  - Freedom vs. slavery.
    - If you sin, you are the slave of sin.
    - If you are a slave, you have no place.
    - If the Son sets you free, you are free.
  - Ancestry.
    - You are Abraham's offspring.

54

- You seek to kill Me.
        - You don't have My word.
    - We have different fathers.
        - I speak for My Father.
        - You act for your father.
- False Security Reiterated.
- His Assessment.
    - Principle: If you are Abraham's children, do the deeds of Abraham.
    - The deeds we do:
        - My deeds: I told you the truth.
        - Abraham's deeds: He obeyed God's truth.
        - Your deeds: You seek to kill Me.
        - Your fathers' deeds: They killed the prophets.
- Their Condemnation.
    - You are illegitimate!
    - Our Father is God!
- His Conclusion.
    - If God were your Father:
        - You would love Me.
        - You would know Me.
    - Since Satan is your father:
        - Satan is the pattern.
            - He is a murderer.
            - He is a liar.
        - You are the product.
            - You do his desires.
            - You are intent on murder.
- His Accusation.
    - "Which of you accuses Me?"
    - I speak the truth, you don't believe Me.
    - You do not hear the truth, you are not of God.

Applications

1. Here Jesus makes an amazing statement, "If you abide in My word, you will know the truth and it will set you free." What

does it mean to abide in His word? How would you say you are doing in your abiding?

2. When the Jews called Jesus illegitimate in verse 41, this was not a nice thing. How could He possibly keep His composure in the face of this accusation, which was an insult to His mother and His Father?

3. Family resemblance is an interesting phenomenon. Do you bear a strong resemblance to either or both of your parents? Your siblings? Could people tell just by looking at you that you belong to God—that He is your Father?

Jesus and the Jewish Leaders. John 8:48-59

- The Leaders Retaliate.
  - You are a Samaritan!
  - You have a demon!
- Jesus Responds.
  - My character.
    - I do not have a demon.
    - I honor My Father.
  - My promise.
    - If you keep my word.
    - You shall never die.
- The Leaders Rebut.
  - Our experience.
    - Abraham died.
    - The prophets died.
  - Our questions.
    - You are not greater than Abraham?
    - Whom do You make Yourself out to be?
- Jesus Answers.
  - My glory.
    - If I glorify Myself, it is nothing.
    - If God glorifies Me, it is everything.
  - My knowledge.
    - I know Him.
    - I obey Him.

- My day.
  - Abraham anticipated it.
  - Abraham rejoiced in it.
- The Leaders Protest.
  - You are not fifty years old!
  - Have You seen Abraham?
- Jesus Explains.
  - Before Abraham was born…
  - I AM. Exodus 3:14
- The Leaders React.

Applications

1. Jesus makes a preposterous statement here, "If anyone keeps My word he shall never see death." Do you believe this? What did He subsequently do that convinces us that He is well able to deliver on this promise?
2. The Jews were really big fans of Abraham. They thought that just because they were related to Abraham they would get a free pass from God—that He was obligated to accept them in heaven. What's new? Many people today are the same. How so?
3. On what are you depending to make you acceptable to God? Do you see that if it is anything, anything other that what Jesus has already done for you on the cross, you are in deep weeds? Your ancestor wasn't Abraham. You aren't one of God's "chosen people." You haven't a thing going for you. You are bankrupt!
4. Some people make the mistake of writing Jesus off as just a great teacher. In this passage He clearly claims to be God and the Jews understood exactly what He was saying. How do you know this? Can you remember where this is in the Bible so you can point it out to those who make the same mistake?
5. Can you imagine the courage it took for Jesus to stand in the Temple toe to toe with the religious leaders of the day and engage them like this? It would be similar to you or me standing in the Supreme Court of the United States taking on

57

the justices over some major issue of contention. One has to admire the courage of Jesus. And when major issues are at stake, we too should be willing to take on the opposition, don't you agree?

JOHN 9

Jesus and the Man Born Blind. John 9:1-12

- The Setting.
  - Exiting the Temple.
  - Passing the people.
- The Characters.
  - Jesus, His disciples.
  - A beggar.
  - The people.
    - Neighbors.
    - Bystanders.
- Q & A.
  - Disciples: "Who sinned?"
    - The man?
    - His parents?
  - Jesus.
    - Man's works.
    - God's work.
    - Our work.
- The Healing.
  - Clay.
  - Water.
- The Response.
  - Neighbors.
    - Is this the beggar?
    - Or one like him?
    - How were you healed?
  - The beggar.
    - How I was healed.
    - Who healed me?

Applications

1. Have you ever heard someone say that some person was sick or suffering because of sin? Not all illness, misfortune, etc., is a

direct result of sin. Can you think of a bad situation in your experience which God used for His glory?

2. What is the significance of being born blind? How is this different from someone who had sight and lost it?

3. Why do you suppose this man's neighbors were unable to positively identify him?

4. Can you draw a general inference from this situation about the difference Jesus can make in the life of an individual (see Mark 5:15)? Can you cite examples from your own life?

The Beggar and the Pharisees. John 9:13-23

- The Beggar's Testimony.
  - Pharisees' question: "How?"
  - Beggar's answer.
    - Jesus worked.
    - I washed.
    - I see.
- The Pharisees' Quandary.
  - He does not keep the Sabbath.
  - He does perform great signs.
- The Pharisees Question the Beggar.
  - What do you say about Him?
  - We don't believe you were blind.
- The Pharisees Question the Beggar's Parents.
  - The questions.
    - Is this your son?
    - Was he born blind?
    - How does he now see?
  - The replies.
    - We know this is our son.
    - We know he was born blind.
    - We don't know how he sees.
    - He is of age—ask him.

Applications

1. The text says that "they" brought the man to the Pharisees. Who do you suppose John means by "they"? Why would they do this?
2. The Pharisees grilled both the man and his parents very thoroughly, asking about the nature of his blindness and who they thought Jesus was. Why were they following these two lines of inquiry?
3. Is there any indication that the Pharisees were influenced at all by the answers they received?

The Beggar and the Pharisees Again. John 9:24-34.

- The Pharisees Perturbed.
  - Give glory to God.
  - This man is a sinner.
- The Beggar Exasperated.
  - This I don't know.
  - This I do know.
- The Pharisees Perplexed.
  - What did He do to you?
  - How did He heal you?
- The Beggar Accuses.
  - I told you once—you did not listen.
  - If I tell you again—will you become His disciple?
- The Pharisees Revile.
  - You are His disciple.
  - We are Moses' disciples.
- The Beggar Lectures.
  - An amazing thing.
  - An anointed man.
- The Pharisees React.
  - Give glory to God.
  - This man is a sinner.
  - You are out!

Applications

1. The Pharisees resumed their questioning of the man, trying to get him to incriminate Jesus. Would it have made any difference had the man agreed with them?
2. Why do you suppose the Pharisees were so incensed when the man began to lecture them about Jesus? Can you see any modern day parallels?
3. What would have been the affect of the man being put out of the Temple? What would have been the affect on his family?

Jesus and the Man. John 9:35-41

- Jesus Seeks the Man.
  - Jesus.
    - He hears.
    - He seeks.
    - He speaks: "Do you believe?"
  - The man.
    - Who is the Son of Man?
    - I would believe in Him.
- Jesus Instructs the Man.
  - Jesus.
    - You have seen Him.
    - You are listening to Him.
  - The man.
    - Believed.
    - Worshipped.
- Jesus Instructs the Pharisees.
  - Jesus remarks.
    - Those who do not see.
    - Those who do see.
  - Pharisees query: "We are not blind?"
  - Jesus answers.
    - "If you were blind."
    - "Since you see…"

Applications

1. How could the man have left Jesus without discovering who He was? Without thanking Him? Why did Jesus seek out the man later?
2. Upon discovering who Jesus was, what was the natural response of the man? Do you recall times in your own life understanding anew who Jesus is and worshipping Him?
3. Jesus was a master at seizing teachable moments and using a specific situation to teach a general truth. In today's English, re-state the truth being taught in verse 41.

JOHN 10

Teaching about Shepherds. John 10:1-6

- Shepherds & Strangers.
  - Thieves. Enter surreptitiously.
  - Shepherds. Enter by the door.
- Shepherds & Sheep.
  - Sheep hear the shepherd's voice.
  - Shepherds call the sheep by name.
  - Sheep follow the shepherd.
  - Shepherds lead the sheep out.

Applications

1. In John 1:1, John identifies Jesus as the Word. Words are used to communicate. What does this simple parable say about Jesus' ability to communicate truth to His followers?
2. It is important in considering a parable to understand the parallels between elements of the story and elements of the truth being communicated. In this parable, who is the shepherd? Who do the sheep represent? Who is the thief? Who is the doorkeeper?
3. What is the main point Jesus is trying to communicate with this illustration?

Teaching about the Good Shepherd. John 10:7-18

- I am the Door.
  - Those who came before, destruction.
  - Those who pass through, abundance.
    - They shall be saved.
    - They shall go in and out.
    - They shall find pasture.
- I am the Good Shepherd.
  - The good shepherd.
    - Owns the sheep.

- Lays down His life.
- Knows the sheep.
- Has other sheep.
- Unites the sheep.
- Is loved by the Father.
  - The hireling.
    - Has no concern for the sheep.
    - Abandons the sheep.

Applications

1. John 10:10 is one of the most well-known verses in the Gospel. Explain (recalling the context of the sheep and the shepherd) what Jesus means by abundant life. Are you experiencing an abundant life in this sense?
2. The good shepherd is absolutely focused on and concerned for the sheep. Name four things that characterize his care for the sheep. What does this communicate about God's care for you?
3. What does Jesus mean by the expression "other sheep"? Do you personally know any of these other sheep? Are you at all concerned about helping any of these sheep who may be lost?

Division among the Jews. John 10:19-21

- Why Do You Listen to Him?
- He Opened the Eyes of the Blind.

Applications

1. Describe how people today are divided on the question of Jesus.
2. What are some of the things people today say about Jesus?

Teaching about True Sheep. John 10:22-30

- The Situation.
  - The time.
    - The Feast of Dedication.

- The Feast of Lights.
- December 23.
  - The Location.
    - The Temple in Jerusalem.
    - The Portico of Solomon.
- The Questions.
  - When will You tell us?
  - Are You the Christ?
- The Answers.
  - An answer given.
    - I have answered you.
    - You have not believed.
  - An explanation offered.
    - False sheep reject.
    - True sheep believe.
      - They hear My voice.
      - I know them.
      - They follow Me.
      - I give them eternal life.
      - My Father preserves them.
  - An observation stated: "I and the Father are one."

Applications

1. In this passage, the Jews ask Jesus to tell them plainly whether or not He is the Christ. Is this a legitimate request? Why or why not?
2. What does Jesus mean by the statement, "No one is able to snatch them out of the Father's hand?" Does this statement give you any personal reassurance?
3. What does Jesus mean by the statement, "I and the Father are one?" Did the Jews understand what He was suggesting?

Violent Reaction. John 10:31-39

- The Jews React.
- Jesus Interrogates.

66

- I showed you many works.
- For which do you stone Me?
- The Jews Answer.
  - Not for good works.
  - But for blasphemy.
- Jesus Responds.
  - I said, "you are gods."
  - I said, "I am the Son of God."
  - Assess My works.
- The Jews Act.

Applications

1. With the prospect of being stoned confronting Him, what does Jesus do? This is a remarkable response. Do you think an imposter would have responded this way?
2. Jesus has previously mentioned His works as evidence of His person. Do you think this is a good tactic? Why or why not? No speculation allowed here.

A Change of Scenery. John 10:40-42

- The Setting.
  - Beyond the Jordan.
  - John's location.
- The Conclusion.
  - Remembering John's testimony.
    - John gave no signs.
    - Jesus fulfills John's testimony.
  - Responding to Jesus' person.

Applications

1. What is John's purpose in including these verses in the narrative? Is this just another "time/place" tag or do these verses give us insight into Jesus' method?

2. In verses 41 and 42, John says many came to Him and many believed. Would you hazard a guess as to what John means by "many"?

JOHN 11

Disturbing News from Bethany. John 11:1-16

- The Setting.
  - Jesus. Beyond the Jordan.
  - Lazarus. Bethany near Jerusalem.
- The Family.
  - Lazarus. John 11:36
  - Mary. John 12:3, Luke 10:38-42
  - Martha. Luke 10:38-42
- The News.
  - The situation. Lazarus is sick. (John 11:1,2,3)
  - The message. "Lord, Lazarus is sick."
- The Response.
  - An amazing conclusion.
    - The illness. Not ultimately fatal.
    - The purpose. For God's glory.
  - An agonizing delay.
    - The delay: two days.
    - The decision: "Let's go."
- The Debate.
  - Danger.
    - Disciples. Judea is unsafe.
    - Jesus. I have work.
      - Walking by day.
      - Walking by night.
  - Diagnosis.
    - Jesus: Lazarus is asleep.
    - Disciples: Lazarus will recover
  - Clarification.
    - Jesus.
      - Lazarus is dead.
      - You lack faith.
    - Thomas.
      - Let us go.
      - We may die.

69

Applications

1. The Apostle John gives us several glimpses of the way Jesus responded (or failed to respond) to urgency: John 2:4, 7:6, and 11:6. Why does He do this? What do these examples say to you about your own response to urgency?
2. In this passage, we again see the disciples having trouble understanding what Jesus was telling them. Why do you suppose they were rarely "tracking with Him"? What about you? Do you thoroughly understand everything Jesus said? Is this bad?
3. Here we see the Apostle Thomas at his best—he is ready to die for Jesus. In John 20:25 we see him at his worst—full of doubt and suspicion. How can one vacillate so in his faith? Aren't we all a lot like Thomas in this respect?

Jesus and Martha. John 11:17-27

- The Situation.
  - Lazarus. Buried four days.
  - The Jews. Consoled the sisters.
  - Jesus. Discerned the facts.
  - Martha. Came to Jesus.
  - Mary. Stayed at home.
- Martha's Lament.
  - Martha.
    - "If You had been here."
    - "If you ask of God."
  - Jesus. Lazarus will live.
- Jesus' Assurance.
  - Martha. He will rise.
  - Jesus.
    - I am the resurrection.
    - He who believes.
      - Shall live, though he dies.
      - Shall never die.

70

- Martha.
  - I accept You as the Messiah.
  - I know You are God's Son.

Jesus and Mary. John 11:28-37

- The Situation.
  - Martha. Summoned Mary.
  - Jesus. Remained apart.
  - Mary. Came to Jesus.
  - The Jews. Followed Mary.
- Mary's Lament.
  - Mary. "If You had been here."
  - Jesus.
    - Saw.
    - Felt.
    - Spoke.
    - Wept
  - The Jews. Asked.

Applications

1. Given their devotion to Jesus, it is a bit surprising that both of the sisters did not seek Jesus out when they heard He had arrived. How do you account for the fact that Martha, not Mary, went to Him? See Luke 10:38-42 before answering.
2. It is one thing to fault Jesus for not preventing some calamity in our lives, it is quite another to express faith that Jesus can bring good out of hopeless situations. Do you see the difference in the faith of the two sisters? Do you have Martha's or Mary's faith?
3. What about the question posed by the Jews? Could Jesus have prevented Lazarus' death? What say you?

Lazarus, Come Forth! John 11:38-44

- The Situation.
  - The tomb.
    - A cave.
    - A stone.
  - The deceased.
    - Dead four days.
    - Decay for certain.
- The Instructions.
  - To the people.
    - Remove the stone.
    - Believe the Son.
    - See the glory.
  - To the Father.
    - Thank You for hearing.
    - That the people believe.
  - To Lazarus. Come forth!
- The Resurrection.
  - Lazarus came out bound.
  - The people let him go.

Applications

1. This is truly an astounding story. Do you believe it happened exactly as John reported it? What are some alternative explanations? Why are these not acceptable to a reasonable inquirer?
2. There are really only two possible conclusions you can draw from this passage: (1) Jesus raised Lazarus from the dead, or (2) John made the whole story up—it is fiction. Which do you believe? What are the implications of your belief?

The Curious Outcome. John 11:45-46

- Many believed in Jesus.
- Some reported to the Pharisees.

The Leaders React. John 11:47-53

- A Council Convened.
  - The facts.
    - Jesus is doing many signs.
    - What are we doing in turn?
  - The conclusion.
    - All men will believe.
    - The Romans will retaliate.
- A Priest Predicts.
  - His criticism.
    - You know nothing.
    - You are naïve.
  - His prediction.
    - From the human perspective.
      - Jesus would die.
      - The nation would survive.
    - From the divine perspective.
      - Jesus would die for the nation.
      - Jesus would die for the elect.
- The Leaders Plan.

Applications

1. It is difficult for us to comprehend how the majority of the Jewish leaders could be so corrupt. How does this situation compare, for example, with the Watergate scandal during the Nixon administration?
2. Read John 12:42 and Acts 6:7. Do these verses give you any different perspective relative to the level of corruption to which the priesthood had sunk? Both verses suggest that "many" priests believed. How many is "many"? No speculation allowed.

Jesus Withdraws. John 11:54-57

- The Retreat.
  - The Characters.
    - Jesus.
    - His disciples.
  - The Location.
    - A wilderness area.
    - The city of Ephraim.
- The Passover.
  - The characters.
    - The people.
    - The leaders.
  - The location—Jerusalem.
  - The responses.
    - The people. "Will Jesus come?"
    - The Leaders. Put out an APB.

Applications

1. John writes that Jesus "no longer walked publicly among the Jews, but went away." Do you think He feared for His life? What other explanation can account for his withdrawal?
2. Do you think the people were at all sympathetic with their leaders? Would they cooperate with them and turn Him in given the opportunity? Why or why not?

JOHN 12

Jesus and the Anointing by Mary. John 12:1-8

- The Setting.
  - The occasion.
    - Before the Passover.
    - At Lazarus' home.
    - In Bethany.
  - The guests.
    - Jesus, His disciples.
    - Lazarus, reclining.
    - Martha, serving.
    - Mary, worshiping.
- Mary's Work.
  - The substance.
    - Spikenard ointment.
      - One pound.
      - Very costly.
    - Mary's devotion.
  - The anointing.
    - Anointed His feet with ointment.
    - Wiped His feet with her hair.
    - Filled the house with fragrance.
- Judas' Reaction.
  - His complaint.
    - The ointment should have been sold.
    - The proceeds should have been given.
  - His motivation.
    - Concern for the poor.
    - Concern for himself.
      - He was a thief.
      - He pilfered money.
- Jesus' Response.
  - Let her alone.
  - Worship vs. service.

Applications

1. Can you imagine the thoughts of the people who were present at this meal? Lazarus—truly living on borrowed time? Mary and Martha—déjà vu all over again? Jesus—only a few days until the cross? The disciples—just another dinner with the Lord; what can happen next?
2. Mary may have acquired the ointment for her dowry; she might have inherited it from her parents. But her devotion to Jesus and her love for Him caused her to see it only as a resource to be lavished on Jesus. What about you? Do you see your stuff as resources to be expended for Jesus?
3. We all suffer from the dilemma of Judas—concern for others vs. concern for ourselves. How many of your decisions are made on the basis of self-interest vs. considering the interests of others?

The Jews and the Chief Priests. John 12:9-11

- The Crowds.
    - Came from Jerusalem.
    - Came with two motives.
        - To see Jesus.
        - To see Lazarus.
- The Chief Priests.
    - Formed a plan.
    - Motivated by concern.
        - The Jews were leaving.
        - The Jews were believing.

Palm Sunday. John 12:12-19

- The Crowds.
    - Heard Jesus was coming.
    - Took palm branches
    - Cried out in praise.
    -

- Jesus.
  - Found a donkey.
  - Rode into the city.
  - Cited the Scriptures.
- The Disciples.
  - Failed to understand.
  - Later remembered.
- The Pharisees.
  - Talked to one another.
  - "The world follows Him!"

Applications

1. Why were the chief priests so intent on killing Lazarus? What had he done to arouse their wrath?
2. In laying palm branches before Jesus as He rode into Jerusalem, the crowds were hailing Him as a conquering king. Was this an appropriate recognition of Him as the promised Messiah?
3. The Pharisees rightly acknowledged that many of the Jews were following Jesus. What would have been an appropriate response to this assessment?

Greeks Ask to See Jesus. John 12:20-26

- Certain Greeks.
  - Converts to Judaism.
  - Connected to Philip?
- Philip.
  - Entertained their request.
  - Referred it to Andrew.
- Jesus.
  - The hour has come.
  - A grain of wheat.
    - Must die alone.
    - To bear fruit.
  - Your life.
    - Love it, lose it.

- Hate it, keep it.
- My servants.
  - Are with Me.
  - Are honored by God.

Applications

1. The motive of the Greeks for wanting to see Jesus is unclear from the text. Can you suggest several plausible possibilities? Which do you think the most likely?
2. There is no indication from the text that these Greeks ever got to speak with Jesus. Apparently they saw and heard Him. Do you suppose they were satisfied with the outcome?

Teaching about Judgment! John 12:21-36a

- Jesus Consults His Father.
  - His motivation.
  - His supplication.
- The Father's Response.
  - A voice from heaven.
  - A request answered.
- The Crowd Perplexed.
  - Heaven thundered.
  - An angel spoke.
- Jesus Instructs the Crowd.
  - The voice you heard.
    - Not for My sake.
    - But for your sake.
  - The hour of judgment.
    - The ruler of the world.
    - The savior of the world.
- The Crowd Questions.
  - We have heard …
  - How can You say?
  - Who is this Son of Man?

- Jesus Responds.
  - The light is among you.
  - Walk while there is light.
  - Believe in the light.

Applications

1. Suppose you had been in the crowd on this occasion. How do you think you would have responded to this astounding pronouncement of God?
2. We don't make much today of the fact that Satan is "the ruler of the world." Do you actually believe this, or is this just some religious mumbo-jumbo?
3. Do you see that it was necessary for Jesus to die in order to become the Savior of the World? What does He mean when He says, "I will draw all men to Myself?"

John Summarizes the Situation. John 12:36a-43

- The Characters
  - Jesus.
    - Spoke.
    - Vanished.
  - The crowd.
    - Saw many signs.
    - Did not believe.
  - The prophet.
    - A question posed.
    - A response given.
  - The rulers.
    - Many believed.
    - Few confessed.

Applications

1. It is interesting that John shifts from reporting the events to analyzing the reactions here. He uses the Scripture powerfully

to explain things for us referring to passages from Isaiah. How well are you able to relate events in your life to Scripture and to come up with explanations?

2. John says that many of the rulers believed in Him but failed to confess Him for fear of being put out of the Synagogue. What (or who) in your life do you fear so much that it (or they) prevents you from confessing, that is, being open and up front about your faith in Jesus?

Jesus Talks about Himself. John 12:44-50

- My Father.
  - He who believes Me, believes Him.
  - He who beholds Me, beholds Him.
- Light and Darkness.
- My Sayings.
  - He who hears and does not follow.
  - He who rejects and does not receive.
- My Teaching.
  - God's commands are My motivation.
  - God's commands are eternal life.

Applications

1. Have you ever wondered what God is like? You really have no cause to wonder. How well you know Jesus is an indication of how well you know His Father. What do you need to do in order to know Jesus better?

2. How well are you following the commandments? Do you know them? Does the New Testament stuff supercede the Old Testament stuff? Which ones are you following? How are you measuring your obedience?

JOHN 13

Jesus Washes the Disciples' Feet. John 13:1-11

- The Setting.
  - Before Passover.
  - During supper.
- The Service.
  - Preparation.
    - Jesus knew.
      - His hour had come.
      - His authority was complete.
    - Satan acted.
  - Performance.
    - Garments laid aside.
    - Towel girded about.
    - Service lovingly rendered.
  - Protestation.
    - Peter. Do You wash my feet?
    - Jesus. You don't understand now.
    - Peter. Never shall You wash my feet.
    - Jesus. It is necessary.
    - Peter. Then all of me.
    - Jesus.
      - He who has bathed.
      - He who has not.

Applications

1. One of the main things Jesus has been trying to communicate to the disciples is that His disciples are to serve. Do you think that at this time they understood? No speculation here. Give some specific examples of their behavior which would support your answer. Did they ever understand? Do you?
2. The service Jesus performed for the disciples here stands for all time as a testimony and a lesson for us. If our Lord and Master was willing to wash the dirty feet of His followers, is there any

81

service that could be beneath you as His disciple? Discuss by giving some illustrations.
3. What are some ways that you can be a servant to others? Here in this small group? In your family? In Your neighborhood? At your church? In your workplace?

The Illustration Explained

- A Penetrating Question. "Do you understand?"
- A Powerful Association.
  - My person. Teacher and Lord.
  - My work. Foot Washer.
  - Your assignment. Do likewise.
- A Profound Principle.
  - The principle expounded.
    - A slave is not greater than his master.
    - A messenger is not greater than the sender.
  - The principle applied.
    - If you know it and do it,
    - You will be blessed.
  - The principle portrayed.
    - Chosen disciples:
      - Receive My instruction.
      - Believe My office.
      - Receive My Father.
    - Rejected disciples:
      - Feign fellowship.
      - Betray Lordship.

Applications

1. In *The Purpose Driven Life*, Rick Warren suggests that one of our life purposes should be service to believers—our ministry—and another should be service to unbelievers—our mission. What is the connection of this with John 13?
2. Through the centuries, the church has been known for service to the poor, the weak, and the disadvantaged. Is it possible to

serve in the name of Christ and not be a true follower of Christ? As an individual? As an organization? Give examples.

Jesus Identifies the Traitor. John 13:21-30

- Jesus Predicts.
  - His motivation.
  - His message.
- Disciples Perplexed.
  - All clueless.
  - Two connected.
    - John reclining.
    - Peter gesturing.
    - John requesting.
- Jesus Reveals.
  - An overt signal.
  - An unnoticed entry.
  - An audible command.
  - An erroneous conclusion.
    - Buy for the feast.
    - Give to the poor.
- Judas Retreats.

Applications

1. The betrayal of Jesus by Judas is repeated again every time someone rejects Jesus' offer of salvation and eternal life. Do you now understand why Jesus was troubled in spirit? Can you suggest what Jesus might have been thinking? Did Jesus love Judas?
2. How can the disciples have been so obtuse? Jesus says He is going to be betrayed. The disciples ask Him to identify the traitor. Jesus identifies Judas. The disciples say, "Ho-hum." Can you explain this? What would you have done in their situation? What should they have done?

Jesus Gives a New Commandment. John 13:31-35

- Glory.
    - The Son of Man is glorified in death.
    - The God of creation is glorified in His Son.
- Love.
    - The Son's departure.
        - I depart soon.
        - You will seek.
    - The Son's comfort.
        - A new commandment.
        - A certain identification.

Applications

How seriously do you take obedience to God's commands? What about this new commandment? Do you think it is important? What are you doing to comply with what certainly weighs heavily on the Master's heart?

Jesus Predicts Peter's Betrayal. John 13:36-38

- An Honest Question.
    - Peter. Where are you going?
    - Jesus.
        - You can't come now.
        - You can follow later.
- A Boastful Response.
    - Peter.
        - Why can't I come now?
        - I will lay down my life.
    - Jesus.
        - Will you?
        - The truth is…

Applications

1. The betrayal of Jesus by Peter is one of the most poignant moments in Scripture. What was the difference between Peter's betrayal and Judas' betrayal? Do you ever betray Jesus in the same sense as Peter did? How?
2. What can we learn from Peter's boastful attitude with regard to our own propensity toward failure in the Christian life? What does one do when, like Peter, we betray the One whom we have vowed and determined to obey and follow?

JOHN 14

Jesus and His Father's House. John 14:1-9

- The Setting.
  - In Jerusalem.
  - At the Last Supper.
  - With the Eleven.
- A Prepared Savior.
  - My Father's house.
    - A real place.
    - Many rooms.
    - Well prepared.
  - My present destination.
    - I go to prepare.
    - I come to receive.
  - Your future habitation.
    - You will accompany Me.
    - You already know where.
- Two Perplexed Disciples.
  - Thomas.
    - We don't know where.
    - We don't know the way.
  - Jesus.
    - I am the way to the Father.
    - I am the way to know the Father.
  - Philip.
    - Show us the Father.
    - It will be enough.
  - Jesus.
    - How long do you need?
    - How can you even ask?

Applications

1. John 1:1-4 is a passage that is often read at funerals because of the assurance it offers that Jesus is preparing an eternal place

86

for people. But this passage does not apply indiscriminately to all people. To whom does it apply? What about those who claim it [or have it claimed on their behalf] to whom it doesn't apply?

2. John 14:6 is universally misunderstood by believers and unbelievers. It is cited to demonstrate that Christianity is really intolerant. Who made the truth claim of John 14:6? What would it say about the character of Jesus if there were other ways to God apart from Him?
3. Should we let people believe there are other ways to God, even when we believe there are not? Do we have an obligation to engage people on this issue?
4. Do you detect a bit of exasperation in Jesus' reply to Philip? Was it warranted? Could He often ask the same question of you? Would He be justified in asking it?

Jesus and His Father's Works. John 14:10-12

- The Words of Jesus.
  - Demonstrate His relationship with the Father.
  - Demonstrate His indwelling by the Father.
- The Works of Jesus.
- The Works of Disciples.
  - Because they believe.
  - Because He is with God.

Applications

1. Here Jesus claims that the Father abides [or indwells] in Him. If Jesus relied on the Spirit of God abiding in Him, don't you think we should also? How does this happen?
2. Do you really believe you will do greater works than Jesus? How could this possibly happen?

Jesus and His Disciples' Acts. John 14:13-17

- Through Prayer.
  - The scope of requests: whatever, anything.
  - The mode of asking: "in My name."
  - The reason for answers: glory.
- Through Obedience.
  - The motivation for obedience: love.
  - The object of obedience: commands.
- Through the Spirit.
  - The source of the Spirit: God.
  - The duration of the Spirit: forever.
  - The character of the Spirit: truth.
  - The presence of the Spirit:
    - Believers. He abides with you.
    - The world. He is not received or known.

Applications

1. In John 14:13,14, Jesus says that if we ask for anything in His name, He will do it. Does the modifier "in My name" restrict in any way what we might request? How so?
2. Does Jesus put a very high premium on obedience? What does obedience demonstrate according to this passage?
3. Jesus doesn't really go into the role of the Holy Spirit here [that is the topic of Chapter 16]. Do you think that Jesus felt that the Holy Spirit was to play an important role in the life of believers? How so?

Jesus and His Presence with the Disciples. John 14:18-20

- They Would not Be Alone.

  - His visible presence.
    - To the world.
    - To the disciples.
      - Evidence: I am alive.

     ◻ Conclusion: You will live!
  - His abiding presence.
    ▪ In the Father.
    ▪ In His disciples.
- They Would not Be Confused.
  - About His relationship with the Father.
  - About His relationship with them.

Application

1. Do you understand that the resurrection of Jesus from death is the guarantee that your death is only a transition into eternal life? Explain.
2. Do you understand why it was necessary for Jesus physically to go to the Father in order for His Spirit to abide in us? Explain.
3. Do you have a sense of God's abiding presence in your life? Can you give examples?

Jesus Connects Obedience and Fellowship. John 14:21-24

- The Principle Stated.
  - Obedience communicates love.
  - Love is returned.
    ▪ By the Father.
    ▪ By the Son.
- The Principle Questioned.
  - What has happened?
  - Your presence is manifested:
    ▪ Not to the world,
    ▪ But to the disciples.
- The Question Answered.
  - Obedience leads to fellowship.
  - Disobedience leads to alienation.

Applications

1. If you have difficulty discerning the presence of Jesus in your life, do you suppose your obedience might be a problem? What might you do to address this?
2. Do you understand why so much is made of the fact that Christianity is not a religion but a relationship with a person— Jesus, the living Lord? How is your relationship with Him doing?

Jesus Connects His Presence and Peace. John 14:25-31

- Parting Gifts.
    - The Holy Spirit.
        - Sent from God.
        - Entrusted with a mission.
            - To teach.
            - To remind.
    - My peace.
        - Surface, vs.
        - Inner.
            - Absence of concern.
            - Absence of fear.
- Parting Advice.
    - You should rejoice.
    - You should believe.
    - Arise and let's go.

Applications

1. Do you have a sense of being taught by God's Spirit? Can you give some examples? Do you ever sense that God's Spirit is reminding you of something Jesus taught? Can you give some examples?
2. Do you experience the peace that Jesus promised His disciples? Can you give some specific instances when you felt His peace?

3. In Matthew 28:20, in what has to be one of the most remarkable promises in the Bible, Jesus promises His followers, (including us), "and surely I am with you always, even to the end of the age." Do you realize what He is saying here? Are you experiencing His presence in your life?

JOHN 15

Jesus, the Vine. John 15:1-8

- The Setting.
  - In Jerusalem.
  - At the Last Supper.
  - With the Eleven.
- Characters in the Story.
  - Jesus. The true vine.
  - God. The vinedresser (gardener).
  - Followers. Branches on the vine.
    - Fruitful disciples.
    - Unfruitful followers.
- Characteristics of Branches.
  - Fruitful branches (disciples).
    - Pruned to encourage fruitfulness.
    - Cleaned to ensure well-being.
    - Nourished by the true vine.
      - Living in the vine.
      - Directed by the vine.
    - Bear abundant fruit.
    - Beseech God for fruitfulness.
  - Unfruitful branches (followers).
    - Removed.
    - Discarded.
    - Destroyed.
- Purpose of Fruit.
  - Glorifies God.
  - Demonstrates discipleship.

Applications

1. In this wonderful story, Jesus distinguishes between fruitful disciples and unfruitful followers. What kind of fruit do you suppose He has in mind here? On a scale from one to ten, how would you rate your fruitfulness in terms of the things you

have identified? Remember, fruit is produced in and through us by God's Spirit—we don't produce anything of value through our own efforts.
2. In verse 2, Jesus discloses that fruitful branches are pruned in order that they will bear more fruit. What do you think Jesus has in mind in terms of pruning? Have you ever experienced pruning in this respect?
3. As we have seen, unfruitful followers, in this passage, are apparently what we would call hangers-on—not true followers of Jesus, but those who hang around for the benefits. Do you know anyone who may fall in this category of followers? What might you do to cause them to see their real condition before Christ and to change while there is still time?

Jesus and the Eleven. John 15:9-17

- You Are Loved.
    - God loves Me.
    - I love you.
    - You are to love one another.
- You Have Joy.
    - You have My joy.
    - Your joy is full.
- You Are Friends.
    - Friends sacrifice.
    - Friends obey.
    - Friends are informed.
    - Friends are chosen.
    - Friends love one another.

Applications

1. Jesus uses the term "abide in My love" twice in these verses. What does He mean by this? Do you have any sense of abiding in His love? If so, explain what your experience in this regard is. If not, what might you do to abide in His love?

93

2. Do you think Jesus was a joyful person? Scripture tells us He was "a man of sorrows and acquainted with grief (Isaiah 53:3)." How can you reconcile His joy and His sorrow? Are you experiencing His joy in your life? Is your joy full?
3. Jesus makes much here of disciples being His friends. Have you ever thought of yourself as being a friend of Jesus? Of being a friend of God? If not, shouldn't you, based on this passage? How would doing so change your relationship with God?

The Disciples and the World. John 15:18-21

- You Are Hated.
  - The world hated Me first.
  - The world hates you:
    - You are not of the world.
    - I chose you out of the world.
- You Are Persecuted.
  - The world's response.
    - If the master is persecuted, the slave will be persecuted.
    - If the master is obeyed, the slave will be obeyed.
  - The world's motivation: for My Name's sake.

Applications

1. Have you ever been hated because of your relationship to Jesus? Of course, we need to be winsome with respect to the world; we need to represent Jesus attractively. We don't need to intentionally antagonize others; we don't need to look for trouble. Do you know Christians who invite hatred? Did Jesus?
2. Have you ever thought about the fact that Jesus chose you? Perhaps you have been thinking that it was the other way around—that you chose Him. But this is not the truth that is conveyed in Scripture. Jesus chose you. You are special to Him. He has a place for you in His Kingdom. Does knowing this change you at all? Should it?

3. Have you ever been persecuted because of your relationship to Jesus? Scripture guarantees persecution for all who truly follow Jesus, "Indeed, all who desire to live godly in Christ Jesus will be persecuted (2 Timothy 3:12)." How much persecution are you willing to tolerate for Him?

Jesus and the World. John 15:22-27

*   The World Has No Excuse.
    -   They know their sin.
        *   I spoke.
        *   I worked.
    -   They react with hate.
        *   They hate Me.
        *   They hate God.
    -   They have no cause.
*   You Have a Helper.
    -   He bears witness of Me.
    -   You bear witness of Me.

Applications

1. If Jesus had not come and spoken to the people and performed miracles for them to see, He says they would be without sin. What does He mean? Did He have to come physically to show them their sin? What about those who have never seen Him, including us? Are we without sin?
2. Do you understand the importance of the Holy Spirit in the life of the believer? Explain. Can you sense the Spirit of God enabling you to live victoriously in a world that hates Him?
3. It is the job of the Holy Spirit to bear witness of Jesus. It is also your job as His disciple. How are you doing in this regard? Anything you need to do to equip yourself to be a better witness for Him?

JOHN 16

Jesus Speaks of the Distant Future. John 16:1-16

- The Setting.
    - In Jerusalem.
    - At the Last Supper.
    - With the Eleven.
- Persecution for You.
    - Bad things will happen.
        - You will be outcasts from the synagogue.
        - You will be killed by the authorities.
    - You are forewarned.
        - To keep you from stumbling.
        - To cause you to remember.
- Absence from Me.
    - Your reaction.
        - You haven't asked where.
        - You are filled with sorrow.
    - My purpose.
        - You will benefit.
        - I will send help.
- A Helper for You.
    - Convicting the World.
        - Of sin. They don't believe in Me.
        - Of righteousness:
            - I go to the Father.
            - I am not visible.
        - Of judgment. Satan has been judged.
    - Indwelling the Believer.
        - Guides you into truth.
        - Speaks what He hears.
        - Discloses the future.
        - Glorifies the Son.
        - Discloses God's truth.
- The Timing.
    - A little while: while I am in the tomb.

96

- A little while: post resurrection appearances.

Applications

1. Here Jesus is preparing the disciples for what they can expect after He has been crucified, buried, resurrected and ascended— for the distant future. What do you think they were thinking about their long-term involvement with Jesus? Do you think that if they knew what was really in store for them long term they would have hung around?
2. Did they really become outcasts from the synagogue? What is the difference between being outcasts from the synagogue and being cast out of the Temple?
3. Do you see a clear distinction in the ministry of the Holy Spirit in the world and in the life of the believer? Explain how the Holy Sprit convicts the world. Can you see any evidence of this convicting influence? Give some concrete examples.
4. Can you see evidence of the Holy Spirit at work in your own life? Can you give any examples of how the Holy Spirit teaches you God's truth or tells you about the future?

The Disciples Don't Apprehend. John 16:17-18

- They didn't understand the timing information.
- They missed the warning about persecution.

Applications

1. Understanding the timing associated with various predictions in Scripture is especially difficult even from the vantage point of the twenty-first century? Is there any indication that the disciples had any inkling of what Jesus was telling them? Had He told them enough for them to be able to figure things out on their own?
2. Had you been in their place, do you suppose you would have had a few questions about being outcasts from the synagogue or being killed by people who thought they were doing God a

favor? Why do you suppose they completely glossed over these issues in their discussions with one another?

Jesus Speaks of the Near Future. John 16:19-28

- Jesus Knew Their Thoughts.
    - They were puzzled.
    - They were engaged.
- Jesus Explains Imminent Events.
    - Reactions to the Crucifixion.
        - The world: rejoices.
        - The disciples: lament.
    - An illustration: childbirth.
    - Reactions to the Resurrection.
        - I will see you again.
        - Your joy will be permanent.
        - You will be speechless.
- Jesus Critiques His Instruction.
    - The disciples' understanding.
        - He questions their silence.
        - He invites their requests.
    - His own communication.
        - Figurative language,
        - versus, Plain talk.
- Jesus Tells Them About God.
    - The truth about prayer.
        - When you ask in My name.
        - I won't request on your behalf.
    - The truth about God.
        - You have loved Me.
        - You believe I am from God.
        - God Himself loves you.
    - The truth about Me.
        - I came from God.
        - I came to the world.
        - I go to the Father.

Applications

1. Jesus now shifts from talking about events after His ascension (distant future) to the time from His crucifixion to His ascension (near future). John tells us in verse 19 that He knew they wanted to question Him. Why do you suppose they did not? Do you think that if one of them had interjected a question, He would have addressed it?
2. Jesus describes how they and the world will feel at His death. Did they understand Him? He uses the illustration of childbirth to suggest that their feelings will turn from lament to joy. Do you think they got it?
3. Finally, He says He will no longer speak in figurative language but plainly. Then He describes what their relationship with the Father will be like from that time forward. Do you understand what He is saying here? Can you translate it to your own relationship with God?

The Disciples Think They Apprehend. John 16:29-30

- You Speak Plainly.
- You Know All Things.
  - We have no questions.
  - We believe You came from God.

Applications

1. Did the disciples really understand what He was telling them after this last interchange or were they just trying to make Jesus feel good? Put yourself in their situation. Would you have felt sympathy toward Jesus for your own slowness of mind?
2. Do you sense something of the Father's patience toward us in Jesus' own patience toward His followers? Would He have been justified in throwing up His hands and starting over with a new bunch of guys?

Jesus Speaks of the Immediate Future. John 16:31-33

- Do You Now Believe?
- The Present Hour.
  - You will be scattered.
  - You will desert Me.
  - I will not be alone.
- Your Present Circumstances.
  - You will have tribulation.
  - You will also have peace.
  - I have overcome the world.

Applications

1. How difficult it must have been for Jesus to tell His chosen men that they would all desert Him in His hour of need. Of all the disciples, John was the only one to stay with Him throughout the trial and the crucifixion. Can you see why Jesus might have been especially attached to John?
2. Have you ever felt deserted by God? Do you believe His promise never to desert or forsake you (Hebrews 13:5)? Can you better appreciate how we can accept whatever life has to offer us with confidence knowing that He who overcame the world is with us and will never forsake us Does this give you a sense of peace?

JOHN 17

The High Priestly Prayer of Jesus. John 17

- The Setting.
  - In Jerusalem.
  - At the Last Supper.
  - With the Eleven.
- The Prayer.
  - Necessity.
    - Jesus needed prayer for Himself.
    - Jesus wanted to pray for His disciples.
  - Conditions.
    - He had shared a meal with them.
    - He had disclosed the future to them.
  - Organization.
    - He prays for Himself.
    - He prays for believers.
      - For protection.
      - For sanctification.
      - For unity.
      - For glorification.

Jesus Prays for Himself. John 17:1-5

- The Time Has Come.
  - The Son is glorified at the cross.
  - The Father is glorified by the Son.
- The Plan Is Announced.
  - Mankind.
    - You gave men to Me.
    - I give life to men.
  - Eternal Life.
    - To know the true God.
    - To know God's Son.
- Glory Is At Hand.
  - Jesus glorifies the Father: by faithfulness.

- God glorifies the Son: by restoration.

Applications

1. Several times in John's gospel, we have seen that Jesus' time had not yet come. Now it is at hand. Can you imagine living your entire life for the sole purpose of dying? Of course, Jesus lived a sinless life so that He could be our sacrifice, but His life has significance for us because of His death. Explain.
2. Based on what Jesus states in this passage, explain the concept of eternal life. How is it possible, given this clear statement, that people come up with all sorts of things one must do to obtain eternal life?
3. Jesus put a very high premium on His faithfulness to accomplish the things His Father sent Him to earth to accomplish. Do you have any sense of what God has you here on planet earth to accomplish? Are you faithful?

Jesus Prays for Believers. John 17:6-10, 20

- The Men You Gave Me.
  - Were from the world.
  - Have kept Your word.
- The Things I Gave Them.
  - I revealed Your nature.
  - I disclosed Your word.
- The Response They Gave Us.
  - They received the word.
  - They believed you sent Me.
- The Things I Request.
  - Not for the world.
  - On their behalf.
    - Those who believe.
    - Those who bring.
- The Things We Share.

Applications

1. Jesus now turns to pray for believers—not just those who were present with Him at the time, but for all believers of all times. He refers to believers as those whom the Father has given Him. In what sense are we given to Jesus by the Father? Explain how the notion of being chosen is in mind here.
2. Jesus mentions two things He has done for believers here: He revealed the nature of the Father to them and He gave them the Father's word? Describe how these two things have impacted your life 2,000 years after this prayer was spoken.

Jesus Prays for Protection for Believers. John 17:11-15

- They Are At Risk.
  - My protection is gone.
    - I kept them.
    - I guarded them.
      - None perished,
      - Save one.
  - The world's hatred is evident.
    - They have kept My word.
    - They are not of the world.
- They Need Your Protection.
  - What You must do.
    - Leave them in the world.
    - Protect them from the evil one.
  - Why You must do this.
    - For My sake.
    - For their joy.

Applications

1. Do you sense that you are at risk in the world? Are you aware of the hatred of the world for the things of Christ, for things which have to do with ultimate truth and meaning?

2. Do you see why it was necessary for Jesus to pray that believers not be removed from the world? Of course, it would be a whole lot easier on people if they were translated into heaven at the moment of belief, but this is not how things work. What would the world be like if it were?
3. Do you have any sense of God's protection in your life? Can you give any instances of His moving to protect you from the evil one?

Jesus Prays for Sanctification for Believers. John 17:16-19

- Their Condition.
  - They are not of the world.
  - As I am not of the world.
- Their Need.
  - Sanctify them in truth.
  - Thy word is truth.
- Their Mission.
  - I have sent them into the world.
  - As You sent Me into the world.
- My Example.
  - I sanctify Myself.
  - They may be sanctified.

Applications

1. Does the fact that Jesus considers you to not be of the world, say anything to you about how you should treat the things of the world? About how attached to the things of the world you allow yourself to become?
2. Do you have any responsibility in your own sanctification? Or do you just sit back and let God sanctify you? If so, what responsibility do you have?
3. Have you ever thought about the difference between God's intentions for you and where you actually are? Sanctification is the process of becoming all that God desires you to be. How much will God have to do when you die, to conform you to the

image of His Son? Is it less than it was five years ago? Ten years ago?

Jesus Prays for Unity of Believers. John 17:21-23

- Our Example.
  - The Father is in the Son.
  - The Son is in the Father.
- Our Glory.
  - The Father shared with the Son.
  - The Son shares with His own.
- Our Unity.
  - Demonstrates our love.
  - Demonstrates our origin.

Applications

1. Jesus puts a very high premium on unity—among believers. Interesting that He desires for our unity to be like that of the Trinity. Are you experiencing this kind of unity in your relationships with other believers? In your church? In your family?
2. Are you estranged or alienated from any other believer or group of believers? If so, what do you need to do about this? Can you see how terribly damaging disunity among believers can be to the reputation of Jesus in the world?

Jesus Prays for Glorification of Believers. John 17:24-26

- My Desire for Them.
  - To be with Me where I am.
  - To behold My glory
- Their Qualification.
  - The world doesn't know You.
  - These have known You.
- Their Assurance.
  - I will keep You before them.

- Your love will be in them.
- I will be in them.

Applications

1. I once had a friend tell me that he didn't want to go to heaven; he thought it would be boring because all you did was sit around and praise God. I suspect that he didn't make it. Can you imagine anything more exciting than to be able to hang with Jesus for all times?
2. If can be frustrating now to know what you ought to be and to be so far from that. Glorification occurs when we die and are instantly transformed into the character of Jesus. Do you look forward to that day? Not as though the bus to heaven is in the parking lot right now, but that someday soon, you will finally reach your potential?

JOHN 18

Jesus Is Arrested. John 18:1-11

- The Setting.
  - The location.
    - Mount of Olives.
    - Garden of Gethsemane.
  - The characters.
    - Jesus.
    - The Eleven.
    - Temple guards.
    - Judas.
    - The Roman cohort.
    - Priests and Pharisees.
- The Arrest.
  - Identification.
    - Judas, the traitor.
      - Knew the location.
      - Led the conspirators.
    - Jesus, the target.
      - Went forth to meet them.
      - Asks whom they require.
      - Identifies Himself to them.
      - Repeats His first inquiry.
      - Re-identifies Himself to them.
      - Requests safety for the Eleven.
    - John, the commentator.
  - Resistance.
    - Peter, the slasher.
    - Jesus, the obedient.

Applications

1. Jesus had a purpose in retreating to the Garden of Gethsemane—to spend time with His Father before His impending crisis. What about you? Do you naturally seek the Father before challenging circumstances?
2. John tells us that when Jesus said to them, "I am He," they all drew back and fell to the ground. The only way to account for

this is that in that instant they caught a glimpse of who He really is and were terrified. Discuss this possibility.
3. We have to admire Peter's boldness while at the same time deploring his brashness. What do you think you might have done had you been present at this time? Does Jesus ever need our help? What does He require of us?

Jesus Is Led To Annas. John 18:12-14

- Taken Into Custody.
- Taken Before Authorities.
  - Annas. The father-in-law.
  - Caiaphas. The high priest.

Peter's First Denial. John 18:15-18

- Gaining Access.
  - Another disciple.
  - Addled doorkeeper.
- Losing Heart.
  - Getting comfortable.
  - Being accused.
  - Denying discipleship.

Applications

1. John reveals why Caiaphas is such a key person in the unfolding of God's plan—he was the one who had advised the others that it was expedient for one man to die on behalf of the people (John 11:49-50). He was the only one who saw the sacrifice of Jesus as a solution to the dilemma of the Jews. How do you suppose he was able to get the other leaders to go along with his scheme?
2. In Luke 22:54, Luke reports that Peter was "following [Jesus] at a distance." This is an apt metaphor of what our relationship with Jesus is not to be—we are to follow Him closely. Do you see how when we allow ourselves to fall away from Him, it is

easier to fail Him than when we are following closely? Can you give some examples of following closely and falling away?

Jesus Before Annas. John 18:19-24

- Questions from Annas.
  - About His disciples.
  - About His teaching.
- Answers from Jesus.
  - Why question Me?
  - Question My pupils.
- Abuse from an Officer.
  - A blow to the person.
  - A question to the mind.
- Defense from Jesus.
  - Wrong response? Explain.
  - Right response? Desist.
- Delivery to Caiaphas.

Applications

1. Why would the high priest question Jesus about His disciples? What did he expect to learn? These guys could not have been viewed as a threat to anyone—they had all split.
2. Why would the high priest question Jesus about His teaching? He surely knew the content of His message—the scribes and Pharisees had attended many of Jesus' sessions—His messages were well-known.

Peter's Second and Third Denials. John 18:25-27

- Denying Association.
  - "You are a disciple."
  - "I am not."
- Denying Involvement.
  - "You were in the garden."

- "I was not."

Applications

1. The individuals who accused Peter were not people of consequence—John identifies some of them as slaves of the high priest. It would be a stretch to think that they could have caused Peter much trouble. Why did he even reply to them?
2. Have you ever denied Jesus? How did you feel when you realized what you had done? What did you do about it?

Jesus Before Pilate. John 18:28-40

- Pilate Questions the Jews.
  - The situation.
    - At the Praetorium.
    - Before the Passover.
  - The accusation.
    - Inflated charges.
    - Dismissed legalities.
    - Escalated intentions.
  - The commentary.
- Pilate Questions Jesus.
  - Pilate's inquiry.
  - Jesus' query.
    - Your assessment? or
    - Others' speculation?
  - Pilate's retort.
    - Am I a Jew?
    - What have You done?
  - Jesus explains.
    - Worldly kingdoms vs.
    - Heavenly kingdoms.
  - Pilate's conclusion—"You are a king."
  - Jesus' confirmation.
    - You are correct.
    - I speak truth.

- Pilate's confusion—"What is truth?"
- Pilate Finds Jesus Not Guilty.
  - Pilate's options.
    - My finding.
    - Your custom.
  - Jews' decision.
    - Not Jesus,
    - Barabbas.

Applications

1. Jewish law permitted capital punishment for blasphemy, which they believed Jesus had committed. But under Roman law, the Jews were not permitted to execute criminals. So the Jews had to find a way to get the Romans to do their "dirty work." Who was ultimately responsible for the death of Jesus?
2. Pilate's question in John 18:38 may very well be the most important question one can ask. How do we discern truth? What is ultimate truth?
3. Pilate tried to wiggle out of a tough situation by forcing the Jewish leaders to decide Jesus' fate. Where did Pilate go wrong?

JOHN 19

Jesus Before Pilate. John 19:1-16

- Pilate Punishes Jesus.
  - Scourging.
  - Mocking.
  - Beating.
- Pilate Attempts a Handoff.
  - Pilate's presentation.
    - Pilate's pronouncement.
    - Jesus' appearance.
  - The Priests' rejection.
    - "We want Him crucified."
    - "We have our laws!"
- Pilate Renews His Questions.
  - Pilate's motivation.
  - Pilate's interrogation.
    - Do You not speak?
    - Do You not know?
  - Jesus' responses.
    - Your authority.
    - Your culpability.
- Pilate Attempts a Release.
  - Pilate's feeble effort.
  - The Jews' fierce reply.
    - You are no friend of Caesar's
    - He makes Himself a king.
  - Pilate's final finesse.
    - The judgment seat.
    - The judgment spoken.
  - The Jews' firm decision.
    - He deserves death.
    - We have no king.
  - Pilate folds under pressure.

Applications

1. Isaiah writing many years before these events said, "He was oppressed and treated harshly, yet He never said a word. He was led as a lamb to the slaughter. And as a sheep is silent before the shearers, He did not open His mouth. (Isaiah 53:7)." Why do you suppose Jesus did not try to defend Himself?
2. Pilate could have easily put a stop to these proceedings—after all he had the full power of Rome behind him as Roman governor. This is a classic case of following the path of least resistance rather than doing what is right. Have you ever wavered between doing what was right and what was expedient? Would you be willing to share your experience?
3. How many people does it take to launch a conspiracy? Pilate, the Jewish leaders, the soldiers, and the crowd were all involved in the execution of an innocent man. What would you have done had you been there?

Jesus Is Crucified. John 19:17-30

- The Place of a Skull. 17-18
  - Jesus went out.
    - Led by soldiers.
    - Bearing a cross.
  - Jesus was executed.
    - Others on His sides.
    - Jesus in the middle.
- The Sign of a King. 19-22
  - Pilate makes an inscription.
    - The charge.
    - The place.
    - The languages.
  - The Jews protest the notice.
    - Not "The King of the Jews," but,
    - "He said, 'I am the King of the Jews.'"
  - Pilate is finally resolute.

113

- The Garments of a Man.
  - Perks of a bad job.
    - Four soldiers.
    - Four shares.
  - Prophecy of a sovereign plan.
    - A problem of division.
    - A solution of fulfillment.
- The Mother of a Son.
  - The observers at the cross.
    - Mary, His mother.
    - Salome, Mary's sister.
    - Mary, the wife of Clopas.
    - Mary Magdalene.
    - John, the disciple.
  - The Instructions of the Son.
    - Jesus to Mary: "Your son."
    - Jesus to John: "Your mother."
- The Death of the Savior.
  - Jesus assesses the situation.
  - The onlookers misinterpret.
  - Jesus gives up His life.
    - "It is finished."
    - Bowed His head.

Applications

1. Pilate finally rose to the occasion, but it was too little, too late. Have you ever found courage to confront a crisis only to discover that it was too late to make a difference? What should we do in such instances?
2. It is difficult to imagine soldiers so inured to the job, that they could gamble for a man's clothing even as He was dying in the presence of His mother and friends. Is there any evidence that any of the soldiers were affected by Jesus' death? From Scripture? From literature?
3. The passage, written by John, in which Jesus commits His mother into John's keeping is one of the most poignant in all of

114

Scripture. What must they have been thinking? John? Mary, Jesus' mother? Salome, John's mother?

4. What does this passage say to you about the importance of caring for family members? Anything you need to do to get your priorities in order in this regard?

Jesus is Buried. John 19:31-42

- Preparation of the Jews.
  - Concern of the Jews.
  - Request of Pilate.
    - Break their legs.
    - Take them away.
- Precautions of the soldiers.
  - Dispatching the two.
  - Dealing with Jesus.
    - Concluding the obvious.
    - Confirming the fact.
  - Declaring the truth.
  - Defending the Scripture.
- Provision of the Two.
  - Joseph of Arimathea.
    - Sought Pilate's permission.
    - Provided the tomb.
  - Nicodemus, the Pharisee.
    - Provided burial materials.
    - Provided assistance.

Applications

1. Recently, I spoke to several Muslims at Speaker's Corner in Hyde Park, London. They don't believe Jesus actually died on the cross. Do you see why the evidence and testimony John gives us here is so essential?
2. Are you a "Secret Service" follower of Jesus as some say Joseph of Arimathea and Nicodemus were? Are you willing to

be identified with Jesus to all of your friends and family members? Your business associates?

3. How big of a thing was it for Joseph to go to Pilate and request permission to remove the body of Jesus? What about Nicodemus' service—was it significant? Speculate on how things might have turned out had these two timid followers not risen to the occasion.

JOHN 20

Jesus Presents a Mystery. John 20:1-10

- Mary Magdalene's Startling News.
  - Mary's discovery.
    - The tomb was empty.
    - The stone was removed.
  - Mary's report.
    - To Peter and John.
    - "The Lord has been moved."
- Peter and John.
  - Race to the tomb.
  - John's inspection.
    - Did not go in.
    - Saw the wrappings.
  - Peter's inspection.
    - Entered the tomb.
    - Saw the wrappings:
      - The linen wrappings, lying there.
      - The face-cloth, rolled up.
  - John's re-examination.
    - Entered the tomb.
    - Believed the evidence.
  - Peter and John's response.
    - Did not understand.
    - Went to their homes.

Applications

1. Matthew and Luke both report that "the women" went early to the tomb; John mentions only Mary Magdalene. Why do you suppose John didn't mention the other women? Does John's omission materially affect his account of the events?
2. John tells us in verse 8 that when he entered the tomb and saw, he believed. But in verse 9 he relates that neither he nor Peter understood the Scriptures that Jesus would rise from the dead.

117

So what was the extent of his belief upon seeing the interior of the tomb?

Jesus Encounters Mary Magdalene. John 20:11-18

- Mary Returns to the Tomb.
  - She stands weeping.
  - She looks into the tomb.
  - She sees two angels.
- Mary and the Angels.
  - The angels inquire.
  - Mary answers.
    - They have taken away my Lord.
    - I don't know where they have laid Him.
- Mary and Jesus.
  - Mary turns around.
    - Jesus is there.
    - She doesn't know Him.
  - Jesus inquires.
    - Why are you weeping?
    - Who are you seeking?
  - Mary answers.
    - Where have you laid him?
    - I will take Him away.
  - Jesus reveals Himself.
  - Mary responds.
    - She greets Him.
    - She embraces Him.
  - Jesus replies.
    - Stop clinging, I have not ascended.
    - Go to the disciples, I will ascend.
  - Mary Reports to the Disciples.

Applications

1. Is there any indication that Mary Magdalene understood what was happening before returning to the tomb? After talking to the two angels?
2. How much do you suppose Mary understood after her conversation with Jesus? What evidence is given that she was beginning to understand that Jesus had indeed risen from the dead?
3. What significance may we attribute to the fact that Jesus first appeared to a woman and commissioned her to be the first witness to His resurrection? Remember in New Testament times, women weren't even allowed to be witnesses in the courts.

Jesus Encounters the Disciples. John 20:19-23

- The Situation.
    - On the first day.
    - Behind closed doors.
- The Appearance.
    - A gift: the peace of Jesus.
    - A helper: the Holy Spirit.
    - A charge: the Great Commission.
    - A command:
        - If you forgive ...
        - If you retain ...

Applications

1. Are you experiencing the peace of Jesus which He promised to His followers? Do you think true believers experience His peace in a general way; that is, in their responses to life situations?
2. Jesus promised His followers a Helper to indwell them, to enable them to confront life situations. Are you relying on the enabling of God's Spirit within you?

119

3. Jesus has charged you to be His witness in the world. Are you faithfully discharging this commission? In what ways?

Jesus Encounters Thomas. John 20:24-29

- Thomas' Situation.
  - Absent w/o leave.
  - Hearing the report.
  - Imposing conditions.
    - Unless I see ...
    - Unless I touch ...
- Thomas' Satisfaction.
  - Jesus reappears.
    - Eight days later.
    - All the disciples.
  - Jesus remonstrates.
    - For the disciples—peace.
    - For Thomas—proof.
      - See My hands.
      - See My side.
      - Believe.
  - Thomas responds.
  - Jesus recapitulates.

Applications

1. How much proof do you require of Jesus to convince you that He is alive, and that He is interested in you and your circumstances?
2. Are you willing to worship Jesus as God as a result of the proofs of His resurrection He has given in His word?

John Elaborates His Purpose. John 20:30-31

- Jesus Performed Many Signs.

- Before witnesses.
- But not recorded.
- John Selected Certain Signs.
  - To show Jesus as God's Son.
  - To give believers life in His name.

Applications

1. Reflect over the seven miracles John selected to recount in his Gospel to convince the reader of the divinity of Jesus. Do you agree that an impartial reader confronted with this evidence would be convinced? Explain.
2. Are you personally convinced that Jesus is the Son of God? Are you assured that your belief in this fact is sufficient in and of itself to give you eternal life?

JOHN 21

Jesus Entertains the Disciples. John 21:1-14

- The Setting.
  - Location. Galilee
  - Characters.
    - Simon Peter.
    - Thomas (Didymus).
    - Nathaniel (of Cana).
    - James.
    - John.
    - Two unnamed.
  - Time.
    - After John 20.
    - At daybreak.
- The Interchanges.
  - Peter and the others.
    - Peter: "I'm going fishing."
    - Others: "We will come also."
  - Jesus and the disciples.
    - Jesus: "How's the fishing?"
    - Disciples: "Not very good."
    - Jesus: "Try the other side."
  - John, Peter, and the others.
    - John: "It's the Lord!"
    - Peter: "Plunk." His second EVA.
    - The others:
      - Dragging their fish.
      - Observing the fire.
  - Jesus and the disciples.
    - Jesus: "Bring your fish."
    - Peter: Brings 153.
    - Jesus: "Come, have breakfast."
    - The disciples: Obeyed, without question.
  - John to his readers.

Applications

1. In Matthew 28:7,10, Matthew reports that Jesus had instructed the disciples to go to Galilee where they would see him. Apparently, not all of them went. Can you explain this?
2. This passage has a message for us on waiting on the Lord. Apparently, Peter got tired of waiting and went fishing; of course, the others joined Him. Was this a bad thing?
3. Fishing on their own, the disciples met with no success. Under the direction of Jesus, they were nearly over-run with fish. Jesus promises that His disciples will become "fishers of men." What parallels between this passage and His promise do you see?

Jesus Engages Peter. John 21:15-19

- Questions.
  - The first exchange.
    - Jesus: "Simon, do you love (agapao) Me more than these?"
      - More than the other disciples do?
      - More than you love them?
      - More than fishing and boats?
    - Simon: "Yes, I love (phileo) You."
    - Jesus: "Feed (bosko) My Sheep."
  - The second exchange.
    - Jesus: "Simon, do you love (agapao) Me?"
    - Simon: "Yes, I love (phileo) You."
    - Jesus: "Feed (poimaino) My sheep."
  - The third exchange.
    - Jesus: "Simon, do you love (phileo) Me?"
    - Simon: "Yes, I love (phileo) You."
      - Simon was grieved.
      - "Lord, You know all things.
    - Jesus: "Feed (bosko) My sheep."

- A Prediction.
  - Simon's life.
  - Simon's future.
  - John's commentary.
- A Challenge: "Follow Me."

Applications

1. What about you? How much do you love Jesus? Is He your best friend? Do you love Him more than anything or anyone else? Is there anything you need to do in order to love Him as you ought?
2. Are you a shepherd or are you one of the sheep? What are you doing to minister to other believers? What could you be doing? Are you just feeding sheep or are you concerned about every aspect of nurturing the sheep you have been assigned?
3. What does the future hold for you? Of course, we can't determine that specifically, but only in a general way. If you knew you would be persecuted for following Jesus, would you?
4. How closely are you following Jesus? How serious are you about following Him? Can you think of any other challenge you have ever had that is more important?

Jesus Challenges Peter. John 21:20-23

- Peter's Question.
  - His distraction.
    - The disciple whom Jesus loved.
    - The disciple who loved Jesus.
  - Peter's deflection: "What about him?"
- Jesus' Response.
  - His prediction about John: Not your business.
  - His challenge to Peter: "You follow Me!
- John's Clarification.
  - What Jesus said.
  - What Jesus meant.

Applications

1. Comparing ourselves with other believers is one of our favorite occupations. God has a specific calling for you. Do you know what it is? Are you faithfully answering that call, irrespective of what others around you might be doing?
2. Jesus gave us as His followers very specific, unambiguous directions for following Him. There is no cause for misunderstanding. How are you doing with the commands you understand?

John Expresses Wonder. John 21:24-25

- John's Testimony.
  - He witnessed the events.
  - He wrote the account.
  - His testimony is true.
- John's Amazement.
  - Jesus did many other things.
  - John recorded only a few.

Applications

1. We owe John a great debt for faithfully recording his experiences with and his love for Jesus. What about you? Do you believe his account is true? Have you come to love Jesus the way John did as a result of John's record?
2. Have you ever thought much about all that Jesus has done in your life? What if you were to write an autobiography? Would Jesus be the leading character or just a bit player?

CPSIA information can be obtained
at www.ICGtesting.com
Printed in the USA
LVHW082329110219
607228LV00010B/289/P